"At the center of any movement of the gospel must be real people who are alive with the reality and ⁓⁓ ⁓f God's love and righteousness. In this book Eddie ⁓ ⁓at produces people like that. The belie⁓ ⁓hat produces a life that is attractive ⁓ ⁓tive because it reflects the character ⁓ ⁓ddie also rightly points out that true d⁓ ⁓⁓ contained in the closet, it must overflow into ou⁓ ⁓⁓ on behalf of others in our communities, including the poor and those whose lives have been smothered by this world's injustices. The tabernacle in the desert gives us a vivid picture that helps us understand and experience a devotional life that is private and public. Reading this book is a journey I recommend you take."

—DR. JOHN M. PERKINS, president,
John M. Perkins Foundation for Reconciliation and Development

"The Old Testament tabernacle was a physical model of the heavenly sanctuary into which believers are now invited to enjoy fellowship with God. Using that model, Eddie Broussard shows us the proper way of coming to God that we might enjoy the relationship with him that he has designed for us. *Beauty in the Desert* is a very helpful and encouraging book."

—JERRY BRIDGES, author of *Respectable Sins*,
The Pursuit of Holiness, and *Trusting God*

"Eddie Broussard has walked through the desert of life and discovered how to survive and flourish. *Beauty in the Desert* is provocative and compelling both in leading ordinary people to a deeper walk with Christ and in its perception of God's purposes through the tabernacle in the Old Testament. With clarity and depth, Broussard unfolds how to live and thrive in a world of deserts and disappointments. I know Eddie and his heart for God. He has blessed us with his deep study of Scripture and practical application to real life."

—JERRY WHITE, PhD; major general, U.S. Air Force, retired

BEAUTY
in the DESERT

**Discover Deeper Intimacy with God
Through the Model of the Tabernacle**

EDDIE BROUSSARD

NAVPRESS⬤

Discipleship Inside Out™

© 2011 by Edmund Charles Broussard Jr.

All rights reserved. No part of this publication may be reproduced in any form without written permission from NavPress, P.O. Box 35001, Colorado Springs, CO 80935. www.navpress.com

NAVPRESS and the NAVPRESS logo are registered trademarks of NavPress. Absence of ® in connection with marks of NavPress or other parties does not indicate an absence of registration of those marks.

ISBN-13: 978-1-61747-158-2

Cover design by Arvid Wallen
Cover photograph by Zeljko Radojko/Shutterstock

Some of the anecdotal illustrations in this book are true to life and are included with the permission of the persons involved. All other illustrations are composites of real situations, and any resemblance to people living or dead is coincidental.

Unless otherwise identified, all Scripture quotations in this publication are taken from the Holy Bible, New International Version® (NIV®). Copyright © 1973, 1978, 1984 by International Bible Society. Used by permission of Zondervan. All rights reserved. Other versions used include: the American Standard Version (ASV); The Holy Bible, English Standard Version (ESV), copyright © 2001 by Crossway Bibles, a division of Good News Publishers. Used by permission. All rights reserved; the New American Standard Bible® (NASB), Copyright © 1960, 1962, 1963, 1968, 1971, 1972, 1973, 1975, 1977, 1995 by The Lockman Foundation. Used by permission; the New King James Version (NKJV). Copyright © 1982 by Thomas Nelson, Inc. Used by permission. All rights reserved; and the King James Version (KJV).

Broussard, Eddie.
  Beauty in the desert : discover deeper intimacy with God through the model of the tabernacle / Eddie Broussard.
     p. cm.
  Includes bibliographical references.
  ISBN 978-1-61747-158-2
  1. Spirituality. 2. Spirituality--Christianity. 3. Tabernacle. I. Title.
  BV4501.3.B756 2011
  248—dc23
                            2011017057

Printed in the United States of America
1 2 3 4 5 6 7 8 / 15 14 13 12 11

To my parents, Mr. Edmund C. Broussard Sr. and Mrs. Consuella M. Broussard — Words fail to express my profound gratitude for your love, example, and encouragement over the years. I love you.

CONTENTS

PREFACE

THANK YOU FOR choosing to join me for this spiritual adventure spanning some thirty-seven years of my life. From a humble dorm room at Texas A&M University through the meager serenity of a Tuskegee trailer park to the lush corridors of Moscow's Bolshoi Theatre, this book invites you on a journey to perhaps the greatest discovery of my life. In the most painful, testing times of my life I found beauty in the desert. An ancient shrine—packed up, carried around, and set up again in an arid wasteland for forty years—turned out to be a living parable.

All along it was intended to point us not only to the One who "tabernacled" among us but also to a new path he opened for us, a path into the presence of unimaginable Beauty and Glory. It was here in this secret place that I found more than a refuge in the desert—I found a relationship that satisfied my longing for intimacy. And it was more than intimacy I enjoyed there. This relationship was itself an anchor and a path of knowledge that led me into an understanding of the Potter and his ways that helped me not to be crushed under the weight of life's disciplines but to be transformed by them. It was a relationship with heaven that made my relationships on earth fully human. And on that path I realized I would never experience the fullness of relationship with the King until I joined him in advancing his kingdom.

In chronicling my journey, I have avoided including notes in the chapters themselves so the flow of thought is not disrupted. While the book does provide detailed endnotes, they are not necessary to understand and follow the message of the book. For a more serious reading, however, I suggest taking full advantage of the endnotes. In them

I make use of the original biblical languages but include transliteration of Hebrew and Greek letters so that readers who don't know these languages can fully engage in the discussion.

For you who are new on your journey of knowing God, I pray this book will ignite within you a new passion for him and give you a biblical model of devotional life that will root your life in God himself. For more experienced readers, I pray that the realities presented here will restore or refresh your passion for God and take you to new depths and heights in knowing God. If this books finds you in a desert, may its message point you to a path of intimacy with God that can sustain you through this time of testing so that you emerge from it a person more alive with the reality of God's presence and power in your daily life.

EDDIE BROUSSARD

ACKNOWLEDGMENTS

TO COMPLETE A project like this while serving as Associate U.S. Director and Senior Vice President of The Navigators was an arduous task. It would have been impossible without the support and freedom given to me by U.S. Navigator President Doug Nuenke and Senior Vice President and Director of U.S. Field Ministries Rusty Stephens. You have been friends and sojourners with me in this work of faith. Thank you.

This project would also have been impossible without the wise guidance and encouraging words of my editor, Don Simpson. Thank you for walking with me, Don; it's been a joy.

Special thanks to our friends Arlene and Andy Elcock, and Arlene's discerning comments on the manuscript. Thank you both for hanging in there with me.

There's a long list that goes back to the midseventies of Navigators who have deeply impacted my own devotional life. I'd like to give a special thanks to John Mahon and Sam Clark, who got me started.

I would like to extend a special thanks to my friends, many of whom I've lost touch with, who were students during my time at Tuskegee and were the community that was an oasis for me through the difficult early months of my time in Tuskegee: Dr. Evelyn Baskin, Geraldine Lewis, Revail McCall, Marilyn Booker, Angela Calhoun (Robinson), Jerry and René Latham (René is now with the Lord), Bradley King, Barry Brown, Chester Martin, Guy Trammell, Ricky and Bridgette Browner, Michael and Edna Crayton, Everett Watson, Darrell and Charlotte Spires, and to my dear friends Drs. Winton and Ruby Felton who were professors at the Tuskegee Veterinary School.

Without the scholarly depth I gained through my studies at Trinity Evangelical Divinity School, I would not have the biblical/theological background to write this work. I am particularly grateful to Dr. D. A. Carson, who not only taught me several major New Testament courses but also served as the first reader on my thesis, which provides the biblical and theological footing for this book. I am also thankful for my second reader, Dr. Scot McKnight, whose Advanced Greek Exegesis course gave depth and substance to my love for the book of Hebrews and gave me the theme for my thesis work.

Finally and foremost, I want to thank my best friend and life mate, Barbie K. Broussard, who has been my greatest cheerleader and has borne the weight of my relative absence during the hours of study and writing it took to produce this work by the mercy of God. Thank you for being my perfect companion in life.

CHAPTER 1

THE HOODED CROWS of RED SQUARE

I LOOKED UP into the snowy gusts swirling past the glare of the red star atop the Kremlin's northern spire. Haunting caws of swooping hooded crows mingled with the dreary overcast sky to mix a menacing brew that reflected my inner pain and confusion. I was six thousand miles from home, standing in one of the most historic and iconic sites on earth, and I felt like a marathon runner who had just "hit the wall." I had left everything familiar to me to come to a new world and be part of a fascinating movement to spread the good news of Jesus Christ in sixty-five cities across the former Soviet Union.[1] It had been a grand time! Moving to Moscow, settling into a flat, starting language study, beginning to experience the excitement and challenge of living in a world-class city, and traveling to Russian cities that only a few years earlier were not open to foreigners—I was entranced by this country.

Then culture shock hit. That's when the map you've been using to do life doesn't work anymore. It took me seven months to learn how to pay the bills without getting my phone disconnected! I'd leave language study and couldn't understand even children speaking to me. It would take me hours to shop because I didn't know where to find what I needed. Life was reduced to two or three events a day, so work slowed down. This was difficult because the demands of my role included responsibilities on both sides of the ocean. Even though I absolutely loved what I was doing, immersed in Russian life as I was, I didn't realize that all the changes swirling around me were pushing me to the edge. Then the final blow struck.

I remember how the day started—the quietness of the morning as I looked out my window on the eighteenth floor of the Izmailovo Delta Hotel. A soft mist covered the river surrounding the Pokrovsky Cathedral below me. I began to prepare for the day. It was the beginning of a major conference with our teams from western Russia, and I was the conference director. I walked into a meeting that morning with the leaders of the fourteen partnering agencies. The meeting took a surreal turn when the discussion began to focus on the agencies' disappointment with how the conference was being led. They also raised a couple of other problems that needed to be resolved, and several of them pertained to me. The discussion continued down this path until at last the group decided that I was not the best person to lead the conference. I was removed as the conference director, and another leader took my place. Now these were men whom I deeply respected, and whom I knew had my best interests in mind. And the issues they were raising were correct. So what was I going to do with this?

I walked out of the hotel bewildered. How could I have missed all this? What did I do to let this happen? Before I knew it I was back to one of my favorite paths for walking with God—Red Square. And there I was, the silhouette of the Kremlin's red star against the dark sky, the hooded crows cawing, and my world swirling in disorientation . . . a long way from home.

DESERTS

Some of the most painful times in our lives are also the most formative. These deeply transforming seasons are often called deserts. They are times when life is not working for us. But it's not only a time when life doesn't work; it's a time when *I* don't work. Perhaps it's a failure, especially at something I'm supposed to do well. It could be a string of events that leave me feeling confused, uncertain, or doubtful. It often includes loss. This could mean a loss of position, status, relationship, or something else. Rejection can also lead to the onset of a desert season. But whatever may happen to cause them, these difficult periods of life are often times when our sense of worth, contribution, love, or security is at an all-time low. The most prominent emotion I felt was disorientation. To disorient is "to confuse by removing or obscuring something that has guided a person or a group."[2] This happens when things that are familiar and comfortable are suddenly removed or seem strangely different or distant. What had guided me was no longer working, and I needed to understand what was happening in my life.

Desert sojourns are among the most vivid experiences in Scripture. Abraham, the patriarch to whom great promises were given, was called by God to leave his comfortable and familiar home and family and go to a place he did not know (Genesis 12:1; Hebrews 11:8-10). It was through character-forging times in the desert that Moses became a powerful leader, giving the children of Israel the Law and helping them to become the people of God. It was in the desert that harsh, life-threatening experiences shaped David's knowledge of God, which guided him as king. The Psalms reflect on many of David's desert experiences during these years.[3] The prophet Elijah was driven into the desert and was so discouraged by his situation that he wanted to die (1 Kings 19:4).

In the New Testament, God's Word came to John the Baptist in the desert concerning the message he was to bear to prepare the way for the Messiah (Luke 3:2). When John began to minister, his life mission came from Isaiah 40:3: "A voice of one calling: 'In the desert prepare the way for the LORD; make straight in the wilderness a highway for our God.'" Matthew introduced John the Baptist by saying, "In those days John the Baptist came, preaching in the Desert of Judea" (Matthew 3:1). When Jesus was born, his family fled to Egypt, to the desert, because of the terror of Herod (Matthew 2:13-15; compare Revelation 12:6). Then when it was time for Jesus to begin his ministry, he was led by the Spirit of God into the desert to fast for forty days and nights. Afterward he returned in the power of the Holy Spirit to begin his ministry.[4]

In Scripture, desert experiences were such powerfully formative periods that they often prepared individuals for their biggest contributions. Consider, for example, Joseph's story in Genesis 37–50. This amazing saga begins in the desert. Joseph's siblings were fed up with their little brother's high and mighty ideas of himself and decided to do away with him. His brother Reuben saved his life, convincing the others to not kill him but to throw him into a pit: "Don't shed any blood. Throw him into this cistern here in the desert, but don't lay a hand on him" (Genesis 37:22). Notice that the Scripture includes the detail that he was thrown into the pit "in the desert." It is as if this first event was a portent of things to come in a downward spiral of humbling circumstances that, on a human level, would ruin Joseph's life.

After they throw him into the pit, Joseph's brothers seize the opportunity to get rid of him, without killing him, by selling him as slave to a band of Midianite merchants who happened to be traveling by. How do you think Joseph felt when he realized that his own family had sold him as a slave? I grew up with a brother and two sisters in Houston, and I did enough mischief to them that they probably felt like selling me off at times! But I can't conceive of what it would feel like to be dragged from your family—*by* that family—and to be sold as the worst form of human life to a bunch of strangers. Now that's low!

Joseph ended up in Egypt, in the home of a wealthy official in the service of Pharaoh, king of Egypt, the most powerful country on earth at the time. There, things started looking up for Joseph. He learned a new language and won the favor of one of Pharaoh's top officials, who put Joseph in charge of his entire household. Now that was a step up from sheepherding! But just as Joseph was beginning to excel, misfortune struck again. He was falsely accused of attempted rape and thrown in prison. And there he was forgotten—a long way from home and with little hope for the future.

Sometime later, two fellow prisoners—Pharaoh's cupbearer and baker—had disturbing dreams, and Joseph interpreted their dreams correctly. The cupbearer was restored to his former post and the baker executed. Joseph pleaded with the cupbearer to put in a good word for him, but two years went by and nothing changed; Joseph was forgotten again. Finally, when Pharaoh himself had a troubling dream, the cupbearer remembered Joseph, and God's invisible purposes for Joseph's desert experience began to emerge like the hidden words on an old page that appear when the right chemical is dropped on them. The purpose was always there, but invisible to the person "in the desert." So at thirty years old, after thirteen years in the desert of bondage, Joseph took his seat as second to Pharaoh.

THE EXODUS JOURNEY

To understand this desert theme more fully, let's turn to the greatest Desert Story in the Bible, the Exodus and the forty-year journey of God's people in the wilderness. The children of Israel had been in oppressive slavery to Egypt for four hundred years, and it was time for God to free them and shape them into his people. But why would he lead them from four hundred years of bondage into a desert? Deserts are portrayed in Scripture as hostile places: "He led you through the vast and dreadful desert, that thirsty and waterless land, with its venomous snakes and scorpions" (Deuteronomy 8:15). They are dry wastelands that are uncultivated, desolate, uninhabited.[5] Yet Scripture is clear— God led his people into the desert: "Therefore I led them out of Egypt and brought them into the desert" (Ezekiel 20:10).[6] When I first read this passage, I thought to myself: *This is not what I signed up for!* I thought I was standing in the line that said, "The Twenty-Third Psalm." I remember reading about the still waters and green pastures but not about deserts with thorns, wild animals, and no water or food.

In the face of objections like these, God's Word says that his ways are perfect.[7] God is good, his purposes are good, and the ways he accomplishes those purposes are beyond our ability to understand or evaluate with the little information we have. In the case of the children of Israel, we know that when God freed them from Egypt they were not ready to go into the Promised Land. God wanted to form them into a people for himself. Two aspects of this formation process are of interest to us. First, God stated clearly that he wanted his people to come out into the desert to worship him. The Exodus was first of all a worship pilgrimage, as he instructed Moses at the burning bush: "The elders of Israel will listen to you. Then you and the elders are to go to the king of Egypt and say to him, 'The LORD, the God of the Hebrews, has met with us. Let us take a three-day journey into the desert to offer sacrifices to the LORD our God'" (Exodus 3:18).[8] God wanted to teach his people how to worship him, because it was in the worship of him that they would learn how to relate to him as their God. As we will see in later chapters, one of the major outcomes of worship is deepening our relationship with God. God wanted to bring Israel out into the desert so that they would learn how to relate to him.

There was another reason. Exodus 13:17 says, "When Pharaoh let the people go, God did not lead them on the road through the Philistine country, though that was shorter. For God said, 'If they face war, they might change their minds and return to Egypt.'" God brought Israel out into the desert to form them into an army that was ready for conquest. Fresh out of Egypt, they were not fully a people, and certainly not a military force prepared to take the Promised Land. The harshness of the desert was the best environment in which to forge this band of homeless refugees into an army. But there's something else. In Exodus 15:3, we see Israel coming to know God in a new way: "The LORD is a warrior; the LORD is his name." The God they had just experienced as liberator was now revealing himself to them as the God who is a victorious warrior in battle. Throughout Numbers and Deuteronomy, we see God building Israel as an army to take possession of the Promised Land.[9]

So God brought the children of Israel into the desert to mold them into the people of God and an army prepared for conquest. And now here I was in Red Square in the freezing cold, the last place on earth I'd expect to find a desert. The dominating figure of the Kremlin wall seemed to give off a forbidding warning that pointed to the season I was entering. But to my left, the beauty of Saint Basil's Cathedral called out to me with a different message, one I couldn't quite make out.

INTERPRETING MY DESERT STORY

Leaving Red Square, I hopped on the metro at the Teatralnaya station and headed back forty-five minutes to my flat in southwest Moscow. Shaking the snow from my boots, I put on my slippers, got out my journal and Bible, and took a quiet seat at my kitchen table. I stared out the window at ten thousand other windows peering back at me. I pondered what was going on in my life, and what it meant. Other difficult seasons of life I'd experienced began to cross my mind. As I reflected on the events of the day, three images came to me and helped me take the first steps in my desert experience.

The first picture is the crucible. A crucible is a vessel that is used to melt substances and produce physical and chemical changes in them.[10] When a piece of ore is placed in a crucible, it is heated until it melts. In the process some impurities evaporate; others float to the top and can then be removed. I realized that I was the metal in the crucible, and God was turning up the heat. And I felt that my life was coming apart everywhere, just as the ore does when it melts.

A second image that struck me was the potter's wheel. In Isaiah 64:8 we read, "Yet, O LORD, you are our Father. We are the clay, you are the potter; we are all the work of your hand."[11] This is a powerful picture of God's hands in our lives. In the desert I feel my vulnerability with every pinch or cut of the potter's hand on the clay of my life. And he often cuts or pinches where it hurts. Recently, my wife, Barbie, and I purchased a car after a three-month search. It was exactly what we had hoped for—an older used car in perfect condition, and even the make and model we wanted. Four days after we bought the car I headed out to run some errands before dinner. Less than a half mile from our house I was slowing down to make a turn when I heard tires screeching and some commotion behind me. Before I could turn around to look, I felt a jolting crash, and my new little car was spinning around toward the upcoming intersection. As the car was spinning I said to myself over and over, *"Lord, this can't be happening!"*

When all the cars, metal, and glass stopped spinning around, I jumped out to see what had happened. The people in the car that struck me were fine, I was fine, but my car wasn't. My heart sank as I walked around the back of the car and saw that the trunk was crushed all the way up to the rear window and one of the rear tires was bent under the frame. That quickly, the car was totaled. The Potter had been merciful with my life, and we were again without a car. The Potter is wise and knows exactly what he is doing. We can't see the picture in the Potter's mind. Every slice, every gouge, every scrape of the Potter's hand is calculated. Every motion on the clay is executed with exact precision to sculpt the unfinished mass into a perfect design for his purpose. In the desert, my decision is simple: Will I let the Potter work on the clay of my life? Will I trust his hand? Will I trust his heart? Will I trust him?

Life in Russia made the third image come alive for me, the props behind a movie set. When I moved to Russia, nothing worked the way I was used to. I had to relearn more than language. From making travel arrangements to planning events with our Russian and Ukrainian partners, life stretched me in new directions. The ways of life I had learned for more than thirty-five years did not work in Russia. This was a new kind of vulnerability in the desert. I was supposed to be competent, know how to get things done, and make things happen. I felt as if I were on the movie set of one of those old Westerns where the hero rode into town, jumped off his horse, tied it up, and headed into the saloon, the bank, the general store, or the hotel. But on the movie set those structures were just facades, the front faces of buildings with nothing behind them but a few boards propping them up.

I felt as if God was giving me this picture as a parable for understanding his work in my life in the desert. The desert was God's way of exposing the hidden props I had set up in my heart to support my life. He showed me a couple of props that had to go. First, I was looking for the praise and affirmation of others in my work. I wanted to do well in my work, and I wanted others to recognize it. When I was removed as the director of the Moscow conference, this prop collapsed. I was not doing the job that was needed as the director, and my removal from the role was glaring proof. How would I live with this kind of loss of face in front of the leaders and the missionary teams? In the months to come, God brought me to new depths, rooting my identity in him, not in the other places I was looking.

Then there was the prop of knowledge. I had invested the previous sixteen years of my learning to help people reach maturity in Christ and see spiritual generations flow from their lives. Then I had devoted the last three years in earning a graduate degree in New Testament from one of the most respected institutions in the country. But there were gifted leaders in Russia who were doing a good job with their teams. No one needed me to provide the things I was trying to offer. It finally hit me: I had placed far more confidence in these "props" than I realized, and now it was time to deal with it. God knocked the props out from under me by allowing them to fail and exposing them as false foundations for my life. God showed me that he wants to be my foundation. He doesn't want me depending on a bunch of undependable, ever changing, and limited props that cannot do for me what they advertise.

There at my kitchen table, these three images of what the desert could mean were spinning in my mind when an unforgettable memory stopped that carousel right in its tracks. Twelve years earlier, during one of the most painful and formative experiences of my new career, I had learned something that changed my life. It was time to take that lesson to a new level.

CHAPTER 2

A TRAILER in a RED CLAY LOT

IT WAS FEBRUARY 1983 when I discovered Deuteronomy 8. I had moved to Alabama to reopen The Navigator disciple-making ministry at Tuskegee University. I was excited. I had just completed an intensive two-year staff-training period in Champaign-Urbana, Illinois, and had been commissioned by The Navigators (and I felt by God) to come to Tuskegee. I was ready to go! The first thing I needed in Tuskegee was a place to live. After weeks of looking, I couldn't find housing anywhere. Then I found a little house to rent, but the heat didn't work. The landlord was so slow to fix it that I had to move out. I found myself in a little trailer in the middle of a red clay lot about a mile outside the city, with my neighbors a good Alabama mile down the road.

Then I went on campus to get us registered as a campus organization. I met with one problem after another and ended up in the office of the president of the university to convince him that we should be a student organization. The Tuskegee chaplain, a distinguished elderly gentleman and scholar, had his own questions about our being there. He questioned my credentials to influence students on this prestigious historically black university, especially because I was not seminary-trained at that point in my life. The long and short of it was that I was asked to not set foot on campus for six months while we sorted all this out.

In the midst of this malaise, my parents showed up for a visit, just as I was unpacking my car and moving my few earthly belongings into the trailer in the red clay lot one mile outside of Tuskegee. Let me help you understand why this was so painful for me. My parents had sacrificed to put me through college. I had studied hard in a premed track with the intent to enter medical school to become a physician. But at the end of my college training, I deferred medical school two years to receive focused development in my relationship with God and in helping others to grow spiritually. At the end of this two-year period, The Navigators invited me to join its staff, and after a few months in the Scriptures wrestling with this decision, I chose to walk away from medicine and into a life of reaching college students with the good news of Jesus Christ and his kingdom. This decision understandably hurt my parents, who had hoped to see me serve God as a physician.

And now, four years later, when I saw the look on my mother's face as she stepped out of the car and gazed at me standing in front of this meager, lonely trailer, it broke my heart. She had just spoken with me about three of my childhood friends who were preparing to graduate from medical school, dental school, and law school, and their parents, her friends, were asking her, "And what is Eddie doing?" I was standing in front of a trailer under the cold, overcast Alabama sky trying figure out what to say to my mother and father. And I didn't have much to say.

DEUTERONOMY 8

During those hard months, I did a lot of praying and fasting and walking the red clay roads of Alabama. And when I sat down to read my Bible, somehow I ended up in Deuteronomy 8. In this passage, God interprets for Israel the meaning of their desert experience. He, the Author, helps them understand their Desert Story. In Deuteronomy 8:2 God says, "Remember how the LORD your God led you all the way in the desert these forty years, to humble you and to test you in order to know what was in your heart, whether or not you would keep his commands." Notice that he says to "remember." God wants them to think rightly about their wilderness wanderings and to remember what is true about God's dealings with them through this difficult experience. He explains five essential realities about their Desert Story that they must understand and remember, and so must we.

First, when God brings us into the desert, he does so to humble us. Yes, God does intentionally humble us, and the desert is perhaps the most effective way to humble us for our own good. To understand more fully how humbling works, look at verse 3: "He humbled you, causing you to hunger and then feeding you with manna, which neither you nor your fathers had known, to teach you that man does not live on bread alone but on every word that comes from the mouth of the LORD." When God humbles us, he breaks our sense of confidence. Our confidence is simply what we are depending on to provide for what we need.

Israel's dependence had been on Egypt and themselves; in the desert they could depend on neither. To break this God went after something that would get their attention. Hunger is one of our primary human drives for survival. If we don't eat we will die. When God withheld their food, he didn't just take away something they needed; he created in them a sense of desperation. The specter of desperation creates a student who is ready to learn. Hunger humbled Israel because it created in them a need so great that neither they nor anything they knew could meet it. Israel had a life-threatening problem they could not solve. They were ready to learn.

"Humbling" is one way God teaches. When God wants to teach us something new, he breaks what is incorrect. Israel was not dependent on God. They would never become his people unless they learned a life of utter dependence on him. They would never take the Promised Land as their possession by depending on Egypt, other nations, the gods of these nations, or themselves. God had to break them of dependence on these. When God takes a student to school, the student learns the lesson! In the laboratory of the desert, God works in us to transform us. It is in the desert that he cuts down below the surface of our actions into the deeper layers of our hearts, into what we think, what we value, and what we really believe. He moves right past our strengths and goes into the areas where our hearts are still wounded, into the places we admit no one, not even God. It is these inner regions of the heart that direct our actions. In the laboratory of the desert, God pushes us beyond our comfort zone right down into the painful truth of what we think, value, and believe. We come face-to-face with wrong thoughts, wrong values, and wrong beliefs about God, others, and ourselves that must change. Desperation causes the magnitude of our need to overshadow our objections. And our objections are based on wrong thinking, values, and beliefs. Now we're in school!

3   God wanted to teach the children of Israel that he was to be their confidence. It was he who humbled them by creating the hunger that left them desperate before God. Then he fed them in that desperation with a food they had never seen before, manna, which in Hebrew means, "What is it?"[1] The lesson God wanted Israel to learn was that in the desert he would feed them when there were no other sources of food. He wanted them to understand that their dependence on the bread of manna in the desert was a picture of the dependence on his Word that he desires from them as his people. God wanted Israel to place their confidence and dependence on him alone, even for their very life.

The second reality of the Desert Story is that God tests his people. Returning to Deuteronomy 8:2, it says, "And to test you in order to know what was in your heart, whether or not you would keep his commands." Testing is at the core of a desert experience. To test something means to subject it to a process that will show what it's made of or reveal other qualities about it, such as how strong it is.[2] Testing is often a painful process because it reveals what needs attention in our lives. The testing of metals, for example, reveals points of weakness that could cause the metal to fail under pressure. If that piece of metal was a part of a beam that supports a building, its failure would be disastrous. God doesn't want our lives to fail under pressure, so he expresses his love to us by revealing our weaknesses.

Deuteronomy 8 says that God tested his people to know what was in their hearts. From the early days of forming a people for himself,

God was concerned about the heart.[3] His desire was for a people who would love him with all their heart, soul, and might (Deuteronomy 6:5-6). He wanted a people who would serve him with all their heart and soul (Deuteronomy 10:12). Scripture teaches us elsewhere that the heart is the source, or wellspring, of our lives.[4] Deuteronomy 8:2 is saying that God is most concerned about what is going on in the hearts of his people because their lives will flow out of the activity of the heart. How they responded to God's testing revealed the true condition of their hearts in relationship to him and in the true depth of their knowledge of him.

The purpose of the test was to reveal the true contents of their hearts, and one thing God was looking for in their hearts was obedience. He placed them in difficult circumstances and offered them a right path to choose that was often harder, less familiar, or just didn't make sense. But he left the decision to them. Take, for example, Exodus 16:4: "Then the LORD said to Moses, 'I will rain down bread from heaven for you. The people are to go out each day and gather enough for that day. In this way I will test them and see whether they will follow my instructions.'" God tested the people's ability to trust him for their daily needs. He told them to get just enough manna for one day and not to save manna overnight, because he would provide fresh manna in the morning.

But some of the people did save some manna until the morning. Can you imagine parents with hungry young mouths to feed thinking about breakfast the following morning? They were to throw out the manna that was left over. What? Throw out perfectly good food, in the desert? What if there was no manna in the morning? They just wanted to be good parents. But their hearts were not yet ready to trust God's word that he would provide for their children. In the morning they opened the manna jar, and to their astonishment, the breakfast manna was full of maggots (Exodus 16:17-20). God put his people in the desert to test their hearts and to teach them to obey him.

We also find that God tested them so that their knowledge of him would grow. Exodus 15 tells the story of the people grumbling against God after a three-day journey in the desert without water. The people were parched. They came upon a spring of water at Marah, but the water was bitter so they could not drink it. Their interpretation was that God had failed them. But he had other plans. He wanted to reveal something about himself to them. God had Moses throw a piece of wood into the water, turning it sweet to drink. He tested the people there to reveal his name to them as Jehovah-Rapha, the Lord who heals. If they kept his word, the Lord would not allow the diseases he placed on the Egyptians to come on them. God tested them to reveal something new about himself.

It was also important for Israel to understand that when God tested them, he did so for their good: "He gave you manna to eat in the desert, something your fathers had never known, to humble and to test you so that in the end it might go well with you" (Deuteronomy 8:16). God's purpose for testing the people was to prepare them to succeed in the future. Israel was not ready to handle the challenges, responsibilities, or privileges of their future yet. Notice how God continues,

> Be careful that you do not forget the LORD your God, failing to observe his commands. . . . Otherwise, when you eat and are satisfied, when you build fine houses and settle down, and when your herds and flocks grow large and your silver and gold increase and all you have is multiplied, then your heart will become proud and you will forget the LORD your God, who brought you out of Egypt, out of the land of slavery. (Deuteronomy 8:11-14)

Testing prepares us to handle the successes and failures of our future.

A third, and humbling, Desert Story reality is that we test God. Scripture bears abundant testimony to the reality that God's people tested him. Just two chapters after the people of Israel experienced God's healing of the waters at Marah, they were back in the arid wasteland with no water to be found.

> So they quarreled with Moses and said, "Give us water to drink." Moses replied, "Why do you quarrel with me? Why do you put the LORD to the test?" . . . And he called the place Massah and Meribah because the Israelites quarreled and because they tested the LORD saying, "Is the LORD among us or not?" (Exodus 17:2,7)

Perhaps the most common way Israel tested God was through unbelief, as in this situation at Massah and Meribah. They did not believe that God was with them. Psalm 78:19 expresses their unbelief in this way: "They spoke against God, saying, 'Can God spread a table in the desert?'" The people of God in the desert questioned whether God was able to provide for them in such a desolate place.

The New Testament has much to say about this part of Israel's history and gives this sad summary of those who left Egypt but were not able to enter the Promised Land: "Do not harden your hearts as you did in the rebellion, during the time of testing in the desert, where your fathers tested and tried me and for forty years saw what I did. . . . So we see that they were not able to enter, because of their unbelief" (Hebrews 3:8-9,19). The people of God tested him through their unbelief.[5] God places us in the desert to give us the opportunity to believe him on the basis of his Word and his character. God reveals his Word, his name, and his character in the desert, and invites us in the hardest of circumstances to take a daring step and place our confidence in his Word, his name, and his character.

Fourth, God provides for his people in the desert. The Lord reminds the nation of Israel in Deuteronomy 8:4, "Your clothes did not wear out and your feet did not swell during these forty years." God's presence and provision for his people are constant in the desert, though they often do not come on the terms his people would like. God didn't provide them the wardrobes of kings and queens in the desert. He could have, but instead he chose a different path for a different purpose. Instead of providing new changes of clothes, God prevented the clothes they had from wearing out . . . for forty years! Can you imagine wearing the same dress or pair of shoes for forty years? God wanted his people to understand that he would sustain them, just as he had their clothing. He also provided water for them in the desert where they could not find it, out of a rock.[6]

God gave them victory in battle in a unique way when the Amalekites attacked. As the battle raged, two of the elders noticed that when Moses' hands were raised in prayer to God, Israel won; but when his hands dropped, they lost. So the two leaders, Aaron and Hur, each took one of Moses' tired arms and held it up so that Israel would win the battle. God could have just sent fire from heaven to consume the Amalekites, but he wanted to teach his people something about himself. Exodus 17:15 says that Moses built an altar there and named it after the character quality of God they had just experienced. He called the altar Jehovah-Nissi, which means "the LORD is my Banner." This then became a name by which God was known throughout Israel's history. God discipled his people in the desert by the way he provided for their needs. He established them with a deeper knowledge of himself through the very things they suffered and their experience of God's provision and deliverance.

The final Desert Story reality is that the Lord disciplines his people. Deuteronomy 8:5 says, "Know then in your heart that as a man disciplines his son, so the LORD your God disciplines you." This is an important reality about God's relationship to us that we must understand. God is a father, and a father disciplines his children. Discipline is not pleasant! Growing up, I can remember when my dad went to the hall closet to get his belt. My dad's belt helped me to face the world of responsibility; there were consequences for my actions, and some were not pleasant. Job says, "Blessed is the man whom God corrects; so do not despise the discipline of the Almighty."[7] Solomon says, "Whoever loves discipline loves knowledge, but he who hates correction is stupid."[8]

The author of the book of Hebrews says that God disciplines those he loves, every son or daughter, but that discipline is not pleasant. Yet God's discipline is not without purpose. The author of Hebrews says that when we are trained by this discipline, it produces a harvest of righteousness and peace in our lives.[9]

The reality is that discipline is hard. Israel certainly felt this. A time came when they were just tired of eating manna. Can you imagine manna oatmeal, manna pancakes, manna sandwiches, manna spaghetti, roasted manna, grilled manna, boiled manna, broiled manna, manna stew, and so on? In the book of Numbers the people hit their limit. Here's what happened:

> The rabble with them began to crave other food, and again the Israelites started wailing and said, "If only we had meat to eat! We remember the fish we ate in Egypt at no cost — also the cucumbers, melons, leeks, onions and garlic. But now we have lost our appetite; we never see anything but this manna!" . . . Moses heard the people of every family wailing, each at the entrance to his tent. (Numbers 11:4-6,10)

This complaining and unbelieving spirit among his people angered the Lord. So he sent them meat. God brought them enough quail to eat for a month. But while the food was still in their mouths, God disciplined them. He sent a plague that consumed the complainers.[10] Again God addressed their unbelief, and Moses': "Is the LORD's arm too short? You will now see whether or not what I say will come true for you."[11] The severity of the desert had narrowed their vision. They had been so frustrated by their debilitating circumstances that they could not imagine how God could provide for them. God disciplined his people to help them to know him.

The desert is a formidable place, a wasteland of desperation. In the biting cold of that dark scene at Red Square, I called out to God in anguish of heart: "Where do I turn?" I was six thousand miles from home, cold, alone, and broken. There, on the gray stones in front of the Kremlin wall God reminded me where to go. He took me back to a common thread that had run through many difficult seasons of my life. I found a gem that pointed the way to an amazing destination. So, covered with snow and downcast, my heart and soul went to the one place I knew was Home, no matter where I was.

CHAPTER 3

TREASURE in the DESERT

SOMETIMES WE FIND things of great value in the most unexpected places . . . like the desert. It was there in the midst of the harshness of the Russian winter in Red Square that I found a familiar trail to an unimaginable treasure. In the desert, desperation intensifies our drive for survival. Our senses are heightened; they pick up any glimmer of hope. Brokenness makes us a ready student, and when we focus our desperation toward God, he guides us to a special place.

I felt weak, helpless, and alone. In fact, it was that very gloom that allowed me to catch a glimpse of light that pointed the way to life again. As I stood bewildered, facing the cold granite of Lenin's tomb, the alluring beauty of Saint Basil's Cathedral to my left tugged at me. I was standing alone and downcast before one of the great marvels of human creativity. And this masterpiece was pointing me to the One who inspired its design and gave life and imagination to the architect who conceived it.

I also felt the warmth of God's splendor in the inquisitive conversation between a little Russian boy and his mother as I wrestled to understand the complex charm of the Russian language. In the midst of my dismay, something else was here, something drawing me to a beauty and peace beyond my own matted ball of confusion.

The sight of Saint Basil's caused me to wonder: *Where do I go when I'm hurting, when things are not working?* Then my thoughts began to line up and point me in a well-known direction. For many years a familiar picture had guided me to God's sustaining presence in difficult times. During my days at Tuskegee, for example, a few folks in the community opposed me and did not want my influence on the campus. It was then that I began to experience God as my "refuge," a place that is safe, where I can't be captured by my foes.[1] The word *sanctuary* captures this idea. It means "a place of refuge and protection . . . a place of resort for those who seek relief: a refuge from turmoil and strife."[2]

Psalm 57:1 says, "Have mercy on me, O God, have mercy on me, for in you my soul takes refuge. I will take refuge in the shadow of your wings until the disaster has passed." Trusting God is not just an intellectual exercise, it is a step of faith that allows me to experience God himself as a place of safety. This is pictured in Scripture several ways: Pavilion, Shelter, Hiding Place, Secret Place, Shadow, Wings, Stronghold, and Strong Tower.[3] These words were not just nice metaphors to make me feel better as life continued to grind away at me. They described something I was supposed to experience! When Scripture says God is a refuge, it means that I should experience him as a place I can go to and be safe. These images of God's presence were like gems scattered along a trail to the greatest treasure I would ever discover. As I reflected on them I knew I was close, but I hadn't struck gold yet.

After stopping by an ice cream vendor in the snow of Red Square, a habit I had developed while living in Moscow, I continued my quest. I began to feel a sense of hope as I reflected on God as a strong tower (Proverbs 18:10), and the possibility of abiding in the shadow of the Almighty (Psalm 91:1). These images were helpful, but not what I was looking for. Then it hit me: I was looking for the image of the sanctuary. From Exodus 15 through Revelation, we find imagery of the sanctuary in all but a few books of the Bible. The word *sanctuary* means a place that has been set apart, particularly by God's presence, for service to him.[4] In both Hebrew and Greek, the words translated *sanctuary* come from the word "holy."[5] This means that there is a close association between the sanctuary and the holiness of God.

To say that God is holy means that he is separate from all that is morally impure.[6] This idea of God's separateness in his moral perfection is central to the sanctuary and carries with it a strong message: Access to God is *limited*. Consider that in Isaiah 6:3, Isaiah saw the Lord in his sanctuary, highly exalted, and the words sung over and over by the angelic creatures attending the Lord were, "Holy, holy, holy is the LORD Almighty." Caught in this scene, all Isaiah could do was cry out that he was ruined and unclean in the presence of such a God (Isaiah 6:5), and he was one of Israel's greatest prophets. The sanctuary was a place God was present in a tangible way, but access to the sanctuary was not a privilege just any Old Testament believer could enjoy.

The sanctuary is referred to as the dwelling place of God on earth. Exodus 25:8 says, "And let them make me a sanctuary; that I may dwell among them" (KJV).[7] The sanctuary is also called the place where God's name dwells.[8] In the ancient world, an individual's name told you something about him or her as a person.[9] Abraham, for example, means "father of many nations," which is something important to know about Abraham, because God promised to produce nations through his offspring and to bless all the nations through him.[10] This was even truer of God himself. He revealed himself to Israel and was known to them by his names.[11] In Exodus 3:13-15 God revealed his name as Yahweh, "I AM WHO I AM." By this name, God would communicate to generations of his people that he alone is God; he will reveal what he wants to reveal and do what he wants to do.[12] This name would also convey to his people that he has a special covenant relationship with them. God revealed himself as Jehovah-Rapha, "the LORD who heals," in Exodus 15:23-26. He had previously revealed himself to Abraham as Jehovah-Jireh, "the LORD who provides" (Genesis 22:8-14). God provided Abraham with a ram for sacrifice instead of his son Isaac. God's names reveal to us who God is, and the place on earth his name would dwell would be his sanctuary.

God's dwelling in the sanctuary shows up in another way in the

Old Testament. The sanctuary is viewed as the "footstool" of God. King David said of the sanctuary his son Solomon would build, "Listen to me, my brothers and my people. I had it in my heart to build a house as a place of rest for the ark of the covenant of the LORD, for the footstool of our God, and I made plans to build it" (1 Chronicles 28:2).[13] The footstool carries with it the idea that even though God is infinite and transcendent, he reaches down to touch the earth and manifest his very presence in the place called the sanctuary. So the sanctuary was a place God chose to manifest his presence in a unique, tangible, and consistent manner.

A SPECIAL PLACE FOR GOD'S PEOPLE

The sanctuary was a unique place for the people of God. As we have said, it is first the dwelling place of God among his people. It was the place his people looked for help, as David says, "May he send you help from the sanctuary and grant you support from Zion" (Psalm 20:2). The sanctuary was a place to experience the power and glory of God, as again David testifies, "I have seen you in the sanctuary and beheld your power and your glory."[14] The glory of God was closely associated with the sanctuary. Like the ominous, fiery clouds that covered Mount Sinai, the tabernacle was filled with a cloud and such brightness of glory that no one could enter it when God was visibly present (Exodus 40:33-35). The same unapproachable cloud and glory were present when the temple of Solomon was dedicated.[15]

The sanctuary was a place where God's presence was manifest, and indeed God himself was there. His people experienced his glory in the sanctuary. In Leviticus 9:23, for example, we read that God's glory appeared to the people of Israel at the sanctuary. We find this theme throughout the early history of Israel; God revealed his glory to his people through awe-inspiring displays of his power in the sanctuary.[16] Then in Ezekiel's vision (Ezekiel 10) we can see God's displeasure with Israel when God's glory visibly departs from the sanctuary. Hope for

Israel reappears later in Ezekiel 43 when God's glory returns to the sanctuary. God's presence, his name, and his glory are seen nowhere on earth more vividly than in his sanctuary.

It was in the sanctuary that David said he gained wisdom and understanding to weather some of life's most difficult and unfair circumstances. The mood of Psalm 73 builds to a crescendo as the psalmist vents his frustration at the prosperity of the wicked. He struggles to understand, but finds this questioning oppressive. Then in verse 17, he declares: "Till I entered the sanctuary of God; then I understood their final destiny." For understanding, God's people could turn to the sanctuary. The sanctuary was a place of worship.[17] In fact, it was the center of the worship life of God's people. It was there that God accepted the animal sacrifices that covered the sins of the people from year to year. (We will look at this in detail in chapter 5.) It is also a place that David says God's people will find true satisfaction at a depth that was just not possible through our earthly appetites: "Blessed is the man whom thou choosest, and causest to approach unto thee, that he may dwell in thy courts: we shall be satisfied with the goodness of thy house, even of thy holy temple" (Psalm 65:4, KJV).

At this point it is important to mention that the word *sanctuary* can refer to several different buildings or areas. Throughout the first five books of the Bible (the Pentateuch) the word *sanctuary* always refers to the tabernacle. This structure was an elaborate tent with its surrounding courtyard and furnishings, and God gave Moses very specific instructions for building it.[18] He received the plans for the tabernacle while he was on Mount Sinai, at the same time God gave him the Law of the old covenant.[19] *Sanctuary* may also refer to the magnificent temple that Solomon built to serve as a permanent "tabernacle" in Jerusalem on Mount Zion.[20] The word may also refer to the second temple built after the return of the exiles from Babylon (Nehemiah 10:39). This same word, *sanctuary*, also refers to God's dwelling place in heaven. It is from his sanctuary in heaven that God looks down on the earth (Psalm 102:19). It is from his dwelling place in heaven that he hears the prayers and cries of his people (1 Kings 8:30,39,43).[21] So, in different books and time periods in the Bible, *sanctuary* refers to different specific buildings or areas surrounding them. But in every case, the sanctuary is the place where God dwells; it is a place where people worship God and experience him, and it is a place of refuge for God's people.

A SPATIAL MODEL

In my moments of desperation during those months in Russia, I needed somewhere to go where I would be safe, where God would help me understand what was wrong and what needed to change in me. I needed a refuge, a strong tower. As we have seen, the sanctuary is portrayed in the Old Testament as a place where God dwells, so it was possible to experience God's presence and glory there. It is interesting that passages like Psalm 90 and 91 say that the Lord himself is our dwelling place: "Lord, you have been our dwelling place throughout all generations" (90:1), and "I will say of the LORD, 'He is my refuge and my fortress, my God, in whom I trust'" (91:2).

So if God is our dwelling place, how do we dwell in God? How are we to understand what it means to dwell in God? God is invisible; he dwells in unapproachable light (1 Timothy 6:16); no person can see him and live. So how can we enter God and experience him as our dwelling place? Proverbs 18:10 says, "The name of the LORD is a strong tower: the righteous runneth into it, and is safe" (KJV).[22] God's name is spoken of as something we enter. How is that possible? What does it mean for a person to enter the name of God?

God gave us the sanctuary as a spatial model of what it means to approach him and experience him as our dwelling place and refuge. Entering the sanctuary was entering the presence of God, the place where God dwells. In the sanctuary God gives us a spatial model of how we enter and experience him as the God who is invisible and without physical shape, even while we are in this present, limited, and fallen world. Remember also that the name of the Lord is closely associated with the sanctuary. So when Proverbs 18:10 says that the righteous run into the name of the Lord like a strong tower, it is the sanctuary that gives us a picture of what that looks like because the sanctuary was a place you could enter.

David, in the book of Psalms, frequently expresses this imagery of entering the sanctuary as entering God's presence:

> One thing I ask of the LORD, this is what I seek: that I may dwell in the house of the LORD all the days of my life, to gaze upon the beauty of the LORD and to seek him in his temple. (27:4)

> For in the day of trouble he will keep me safe in his dwelling; he will hide me in the shelter of his tabernacle. (27:5)

> In the shelter of your presence you hide them from the intrigues of men; in your dwelling you keep them safe from accusing tongues. (31:20)

> I will dwell in thy tabernacle for ever: I will take refuge in the covert of thy wings. (61:4, ASV)

> I have seen you in the sanctuary and beheld your power and your glory. (63:2)

> Till I entered the sanctuary of God; then I understood their final destiny. (73:17)

> Splendor and majesty are before him; strength and glory are in his sanctuary. (96:6)

Notice that the imagery of these verses is spatial. There is a "place" David wanted to dwell; it was in the very presence of God, in the physical space of the sanctuary. And it was the sanctuary that gave David access to God himself. The sanctuary was a real place where God dwelt on earth, but it was also a model of God's heavenly dwelling that taught Israel how to approach him.[23] A spatial model allows me to experience something, and experience is not limited to the dimension of ideas. The sanctuary is a spatial model that engages our emotions, our feelings, our longings, our hopes and dreams. It confronts our will and brings us to a place of decision. It challenges how we think and what we value down deep in our hearts. The sanctuary grabs us with beauty and not just information. It inspires us more than commands us. It allures us more than compels us. It draws us more than pushes us. The sanctuary gives us not only the dwelling place of God but also the path into it.

THE TREASURE IN THE DESERT

I was a junior at Texas A&M University when I discovered a treasure that would take me on a thirty-three-year journey — one that continues to this day with the same intensity and intrigue. On that spring day in College Station, Texas, I came across a little book by Jim Downing called *Meditation*. In that book Jim speaks about the tabernacle in the desert in a way that captured my imagination.[24] The tabernacle was the one place on the face of the earth where God regularly manifested his presence with his people. He gave them a whole system of sacrifices and offerings, a priesthood, and a courtyard with an elaborate sanctuary to show his people how to approach him in worship.

I began to study everything I could find on the subject, beginning with the book of Exodus where it appeared. When I came to the New Testament, I discovered the book of Hebrews, still my favorite book in the Bible. The book of Hebrews sparked my interest by showing me how to understand the tabernacle in the desert through the sacrifice and ministry of Jesus as our High Priest. It also explained the new covenant, which Jesus instituted with his blood. The writer of Hebrews did not discuss the temple; he discusses the tabernacle. The temple in the Old Testament was associated with King David and his son Solomon and their reigns. The tabernacle was associated with Moses, the giving of the Law, and the old covenant. For his inspired purposes, the author of Hebrews chose the tabernacle, so that's where I focused my attention.

I studied the tabernacle for the next three years with everyone I was mentoring spiritually in Texas and Illinois. Then I moved to Tuskegee, where what I had been studying was tested on the lonely red clay lot where my trailer home sat. It was in Tuskegee that I began to experience the tabernacle as a model of God's presence, and the pathway into it. This was a way I could enter communion with God Almighty whether I was in Tuskegee or College Station or anywhere else on earth. My earthly location was never a problem because wherever I was, God was already there. That was not the problem; the question was: How do I connect deeply with God wherever I am, especially in the desert? It was in my Tuskegee experience that I found the tabernacle to be an awe-inspiring picture of the beauty and power of God's presence, and the path I could use to enter it. I left Tuskegee and entered nine years of fruitful ministry and theological education that took my understanding of the tabernacle and its meaning to a new depth. By the time I next entered the desert—this time in Moscow—this God-given model of approaching him would guide me through the most intense period of disorientation and brokenness I'd ever experienced.

Deserts in life are inevitable, but being destroyed by them is not. In fact, we can discover some of life's greatest treasures in the desert. It was there that I found a pearl of great price—a way to meet with the God of the universe, experience the power and beauty of his presence, and receive the kind of correction and instruction for life that works. But, again, one of the major messages of the tabernacle is that access to God's presence is limited. At Sinai the people were restricted from coming too close to the mountain where God was present (Exodus 19:20-24). The people of Israel were wary about coming into God's presence: "When the people saw the thunder and lightning and heard the trumpet and saw the mountain in smoke, they trembled with fear. They stayed at a distance and said to Moses, 'Speak to us yourself and we will listen. But do not have God speak to us or we will die'" (Exodus 20:18-19).

Awe is one consistent response to God that we see in Scripture. Awe is an overpowering sense of reverent fear and wonder that is inspired by observing the grandeur, power, authority, or beauty of person, place, or thing. When Moses met God in the burning bush, he removed his sandals and hid his face from God (Exodus 3:5-6). Indeed, Scripture declares that no one can see God and live.[25] So how can we approach a God whose very nature is holy, holy, holy?

This is where the author of the book of Hebrews sets a banquet table for us. People may approach God, but on his terms, not theirs. The old covenant gave God's people a way of relating to him and maintaining their relationship with him. But there was a problem with the old covenant. People were still kept at a distance from God. Something very special happened with Jesus Christ. God came to earth in the person of his Son, Jesus, and forged a whole new relationship with us, on a far more perfect foundation. This new relationship is the basis for our drawing near to God, and to understand it we must go to the book of Hebrews.

CHAPTER 4

PASSPORT to an UNSHAKABLE KINGDOM

WE WERE CREATED to enjoy being awed by beauty and excellence. Whether it's the performance of an Olympic gymnast or the grandeur of rugged mountain peaks, the "oohs" and "aahs" come out so easily when we behold the beauty and power of nature, a stunning work of art, or a magnificent performance by an actor, athlete, or musician. Something deep within us is awakened and we feel alive. Ecclesiastes 3:11 says, "He has also set eternity in the hearts of men; yet they cannot fathom what God has done from beginning to end." God has placed within each human being an impulse[1] that draws us beyond the limits of our time and space to something greater and more perfect.

In the midst of my desert experience in Russia, the beauty of golden onion-domed cathedrals against the blue sky of the peasant countryside and the plush elegance of the Bolshoi Theatre pointed me beyond my gloom. The themes of beauty, glory, and power guided me to one place I knew I could find them, the sanctuary: "I have seen you in the sanctuary and beheld your power and your glory" (Psalm 63:2). That's what I wanted! To experience God's presence with such vividness that the vision of his power and glory surrounding me would alter the way I perceive the world around me. But how could I find this place of amazing beauty and glory? And if I did, what would make it accessible to me?

THE SANCTUARY IMAGERY OF HEBREWS

It was in the pages of the book of Hebrews that I found satisfaction for my aching yearning to experience the beauty and glory of God. Hebrews blends a fascinating gallery of themes to produce an extraordinary picture of Christ and the relationship with God he makes possible. We surveyed Old Testament sanctuary imagery in chapter 3, looking at the unique places and vivid experiences where God met with his people. They range from the simple altars of Job (Job 1:5) and Abraham (Genesis 22:9) to the austere beauty of the tabernacle in the desert to the magnificent temple of Solomon.[2] When we turn to the New Testament, the book of Hebrews is the crown jewel of its sanctuary imagery.

In Hebrews 2:17 the book introduces the imagery of the tabernacle by presenting Jesus Christ as High Priest of the people of God. This is the only book in the New Testament that presents the ministry of Jesus as High Priest,[3] and this is a theme that occupies much of the central section of Hebrews. In Hebrews 4:14–10:18 the priesthood of Jesus is compared to that of the old covenant. The book goes on to give the reader the most elaborate description of the old covenant tabernacle and its ministry in the New Testament. The high priest's ministry in and around the tabernacle provides a way to compare the ministry of Jesus as the new covenant High Priest with that of the high priests of the old covenant (chapters 5 and 7).

In chapter 8, the discussion is taken to new heights when the author of Hebrews reveals that the Old Testament tabernacle was actually a model of the heavenly sanctuary where God himself dwells. Then in chapter 9, the author gives a detailed description of the interior of the tabernacle and uses it to describe why the sacrifice of Jesus was superior to those of the previous covenant. Chapter 10 continues these themes by comparing the old covenant sacrifices in the tabernacle to the perfect sacrifice of Jesus.

Hebrews 10:19-25 is pivotal for us; the author uses the tabernacle imagery to describe how believers can approach God because of a new relationship. In chapter 12, the sanctuary imagery reappears (verses 18-24), this time setting up the epistle's climax where Jesus is again hailed mediator of a new covenant.[4] The book of Hebrews closes with the sanctuary imagery helping the reader to understand the superiority of the sacrifice of Christ and its benefits to him or her in worship and life (13:9-16). The few other New Testament references to the old covenant sanctuary and its ministry pale in comparison to the richness we see in Hebrews.[5]

A NEW COVENANT

The book of Hebrews presents the theme of the new covenant in a way no other New Testament book does, and some commentators say it is the key to understanding the epistle.[6] First, Hebrews is the only New Testament book to quote the new covenant prophecy from Jeremiah (31:31-34).[7] Although there are a few allusions to the new covenant in the New Testament,[8] only the book of Hebrews quotes Jeremiah's prophecy, and it does so twice, in Hebrews 8:8-12 and 10:16-17. This is important for us because the concept of covenant is about relationship. A covenant is an agreement between two or more people that is "usually formal, solemn, and intended as binding."[9] When Barbie and I were married, we made a covenant that established a new marital bond between two very different and distinct lives. Our marriage covenant created a new relationship between Barbie and me with both privileges and responsibilities on the day we said, "I do."

In the old covenant God established his relationship with his people by giving them a Law, which created a culture, a society, and a way of life. The Law also gave them an elaborate system of worship in the tabernacle, including a priesthood to preside over it. It was at the old covenant tabernacle that the Israelites maintained a right relationship with God through ceremonial offerings that covered their sin and restored their relationship with God and each other.

But Hebrews tells us that the old covenant had a problem.[10] The way of access to God's presence for the worshipper was closed in the old covenant. Only the perfect sacrifice of Jesus, establishing a new covenant, could take away sin and cleanse the sinner for a whole new quality of relationship with God.[11] We may now enter God's presence because we have a new covenant "passport," if you will, which makes us citizens of his unshakeable kingdom (12:28) and children in his family (2:10-17), a passport stamped with the seal of the Spirit in the blood of the Son. With this passport we may enter his presence because of the new relationship, corporately as citizens and personally as children.

Let's look at the new covenant relationship[12] with God that Christ made possible. As we mentioned earlier, the Jeremiah 31 quotation of the new covenant appears twice in the book of Hebrews. In Hebrews 8:8-12, the author quotes Jeremiah's new covenant prophecy to explain that the old covenant is being replaced by the new. The new covenant introduces four blessings that create for the believer[13] a very different relationship than was possible under the first covenant. Hebrews 8:10 says, "I will put my laws in their minds and write them on their hearts" (see also Jeremiah 31:33).

In the new covenant, the Law is not written on tables of stone as in the first covenant.[14] This was precisely the problem. Jeremiah 17:1 says, "Judah's sin is engraved with an iron tool, inscribed with a flint point, on the tablets of their hearts and on the horns of their altars." So then Jeremiah 17:9 concludes, "The heart is deceitful above all things and beyond cure. Who can understand it?" The problem was the condition of the heart. In the old covenant the Law was written externally on tables of stone, and the people were to look at the commandments etched in stone and obey God from their hearts. God has always wanted his people to love him with all their heart, not just with lip service.[15] But Jeremiah says that sin was engraved on their hearts, so that even though the Law pointed them to righteousness, the condition of their hearts prevented them from doing it.

The Law gave them a standard they could not keep and made them, and the whole world with them, guilty before God.[16] The Law did not provide for them a way to keep it. The new covenant goes to the root of the problem; it changes the heart! The solution was to take the Law, which was external, and place it internally on the tablets of our hearts, thus changing our hearts. One scholar says the Law is "the kernel and essence of the relationship instituted between the Lord and his people."[17] The solution, then, for the problem of the first covenant was to give new covenant believers a new heart by writing the law of God on their hearts. This theme of "a new heart" can be seen in the major Old Testament prophets, and into the New Testament.[18]

The second new covenant blessing establishes a unique relationship between God and his people: "I will be their God, and they will be my people" (Hebrews 8:10; Jeremiah 31:33). In the earlier chapters of Hebrews, when the author first presents Christ as High Priest (2:17; 3:1), he presents new covenant believers as members of the same family as Jesus.[19] No old covenant, believer would ever think of calling himself a son of God, but Jesus brings his followers into this quality of intimate relationship with God. The third and fourth new covenant blessings unveil further benefits of this new relationship with God.

Hebrews 8:11 says, "No longer will a man teach his neighbor, or a man his brother, saying, 'Know the Lord,' because they will all know me, from the least of them to the greatest" (see also Jeremiah 31:34). The third new covenant blessing is immediate and personal knowledge of God. Under the old covenant, the knowledge of God was mediated through the prophets, priests, and at times the kings.[20] The knowledge spoken of here is not mere theoretical knowledge, but experiential knowledge accompanied by moral responsibility.[21] The knowledge of God in the Old Testament was often gained by experiencing his marvelous works. When Israel experienced the plagues in Egypt, they came to know God more fully.[22] We can see this theme of knowing God through experience in other passages like 1 Kings 20:13,28 and Isaiah 49:23 that contain the refrain, "Then you will know that I am the LORD." In other words, after they have experienced the hand of God, they will know him.

The final new covenant blessing is permanent forgiveness and the removal of sin: "I will forgive their wickedness and will remember their sins no more" (Hebrews 8:12; Jeremiah 31:34). In the new covenant, God highlights the finality of our forgiveness; he no longer remembers our sins. This new covenant blessing we also unpack more in the next section.

We find a second abbreviated quotation of the new covenant prophecy in Hebrews 10:16-17. Here the author summarizes the new covenant prophecy by quoting only the first (the law in their hearts) and last (permanent forgiveness) of the four blessings. The two Jeremiah quotations work like bookends to enclose a detailed explanation of the sanctuary imagery in light of the earthly ministry of Jesus Christ (9:1–10:14). This clever use of "bookends" to tie together the big ideas of covenant and sanctuary imagery in Hebrews gives us a clue to the author's untold scheme that weaves its way through the book's storyline.

A CORD OF TWO STRANDS

The author of Hebrews does something very interesting with these two themes of the tabernacle imagery and the new covenant that helps the ordinary person uncover the path into the very presence of God. By blending these two themes throughout the central part of the epistle, the author prepares the reader to understand the new quality of experiencing God made possible by the high priestly ministry of Jesus.[23] He does this by using the rich metaphorical language of the tabernacle, its priesthood, and sacrifices as a model[24] upon which he can hang the meaning and significance of the new covenant relationship for followers of Jesus Christ.

Let me explain it this way: When I shop for clothing with my wife, Barbie, we usually see smartly dressed mannequins in the store. These lifeless human forms provide a model of what the clothing will (hopefully!) look like when I wear it. The employees dress the mannequins so that I can see how the clothing might look on me. This is what the tabernacle imagery does for the new covenant. The model (tabernacle imagery) provides a form and context so that we can see more clearly what our new covenant relationship with God looks like when we "wear it." Of all the ways God could have chosen to explain the new covenant relationship to us, he led the author of Hebrews to the beautiful imagery of the tabernacle to express the depth and detail of our new relationship with God in Jesus Christ. The tabernacle imagery is the model providing the lush picture to describe metaphorically our new relationship with God.

How does the author of Hebrews blend the sanctuary imagery and the new covenant to create an alluring picture of God's very presence that is accessible? Let's briefly consider three ingenious moves the author makes to connect these themes. First, even though the new covenant is not mentioned until Hebrews 7:22, we feel its influence as early as chapter 1. The new covenant is the basis for the author's comparing Jesus with three earlier forms of God's revelation through: (1) the angels (1:5–2:4), (2) Moses (3:1–4:13), and (3) the priesthood of the old covenant (4:14–5:10; 7:1-28).[25]

Second, the book of Hebrews weaves together the themes of law, covenant, and priesthood in a way that allows the author to express the new covenant in terms of the tabernacle imagery. Notice first that in Hebrews, the Law is limited to ordinances regarding the priesthood and its ministry in the tabernacle area.[26] In fact, the Law and the priesthood were so integrally tied together that when Jesus appeared as a "new high priest" who was not from the tribe of Levi, the Law had to be changed (Hebrews 7:11-14).[27] The Law was even referred to as "the Book of the Covenant" (Exodus 24:7). So we can see again that although the word *covenant* does not appear in the text of Hebrews up to this point, it is clearly the underlying foundation for this discussion of Law and priesthood and the previous comparisons of Jesus to earlier, incomplete forms of revelation through angels, Moses, and the priesthood of Aaron.

Third, in Hebrews 8 we reach the pinnacle of the author's explanation of Christ's superior high priesthood.[28] He tells us that the location of the ministry of Jesus is not earth, but heaven itself (8:1-5). We discover that the earthly tabernacle (of the old covenant) was a model of the true tabernacle in heaven where God dwells (8:2,5). Moses saw the heavenly tabernacle from Mount Sinai, and God instructed the Israelite leader to build an earthly counterpart to his heavenly dwelling. The earthly tabernacle, then, is not just an arbitrary place designated for God to dwell; it is a place for God to dwell on earth that is patterned after God's actual dwelling place in heaven. The earthly tabernacle, then, is a "copy and shadow of what is in heaven."[29] Because the ministry of Jesus is in heaven, it is superior to that of the old covenant. Therefore Jesus, the new High Priest, is the mediator of a new covenant,[30] which is based on better promises. Thus, this blend of covenant and sanctuary imagery reaches its climax in Hebrews 8 where the new covenant quotation (verses 7-12) and the location of Jesus' high priestly ministry (heaven, verses 1-6) are given.

HEBREWS 9:1–10:18

Now that we've seen how the author combined the two themes of covenant and sanctuary imagery in the first eight chapters of the epistle of Hebrews, let's look at how he uses that imagery to explain the believer's new covenant relationship with God. We will look at this in two steps. First, Hebrews 9:1–10:18 explains how Christ's death establishes a new covenant, which prepares the way for a new quality of relationship with God. Second, we will look at Hebrews 10:19-25 to uncover this new quality of relationship.

When we come to Hebrews 9, the tabernacle imagery surrounds us as the author explains the benefits of the superior new covenant relationship for followers of Jesus Christ. The once-for-all sacrifice of Jesus, which establishes the new covenant, not only takes away sin but also cleanses the worshipper at the level of his or her conscience, something impossible under the old covenant.[31] This new level of perfection[32] makes possible a whole new level of access to God.

And that's what I needed during those lonely days in Moscow. I had worked as hard as I could my first year in Russia, and still hit the disappointing wall of failure six thousand miles from home. I needed more of God, and it became clear that he wanted more of me. But what did that mean? The beauty of Saint Basil's Cathedral teased me with a glimmer of hope. Its colorful spires pointed heavenward, reminding me there was a new way to heaven's throne room.

HEBREWS 10:19-25

The tabernacle was a place of restricted access. Only the priests could enter it, and they could enter only the first compartment, the Holy Place.[33] The high priest himself was allowed to enter the Holiest of All only once a year (Hebrews 9:7; Leviticus 16:34). So to have any access to the tabernacle an Israelite had to be a priest. The Israelites were afraid to approach God and draw near to him. They actually told Moses to go to God on their behalf because they were afraid to come close enough to God to hear him speaking to them (Exodus 20:18-21). Later, two sons of Aaron, the first high priest, were burned to death with fire from the Lord when they offered incense to the Lord improperly.[34] The conditions for access to God under the old covenant were stringent, and the consequences for violating them severe.

The new covenant in Jesus Christ changed this situation dramatically. Matthew, Mark, and Luke all record that upon Christ's death the veil in the temple split in two from top to bottom.[35] Hebrews 10:19-21 lays out the significance of this extraordinary event when it expresses the greatest privilege of the new covenant:[36] "Therefore, brothers, . . . we have confidence to enter the Most Holy Place by the blood of Jesus, by a new and living way opened for us through the curtain, that is, his body, and . . . we have a great priest over the house of God." In the new covenant, confidence to enter the Holiest of All replaces fear to approach God. The way into the Holiest of All is new in that it never before existed in the history of God's saving works in humanity. It removed the system of barriers, which restricted access to God, by the offering of a perfect sacrifice. The way into the Most Holy Place is "living" because it exists in a living relationship with our great High Priest.[37]

It was to this reality that the apostle John pointed in John 14:1-6, which culminates in Jesus' stunning revelation, "I am the way and the truth and the life. No one comes to the Father except through me" (verse 6). Jesus opened the way to the Father; in fact, he himself is the way to the presence of the Father. Having completed his earthly ministry as High Priest, Jesus took his seat on the right hand of majesty.[38] The new and living Way is now open through the sacrifice of Jesus[39] into the Holiest of All, a path that was closed under the old covenant.

This is the picture of the new covenant relationship the author of Hebrews wants us to see. It is a picture made possible by the model of the tabernacle. He wants us to understand that the way into the Holiest of All was blocked under penalty of death, until the great High Priest appeared. The sacrifice of Jesus drew a line in the sand of salvation history, making possible what was previously unthinkable. Followers of Jesus Christ would now enjoy access into a place where God's very presence dwells by the new covenant in his blood. But what is this place, and what does entrance into the Most Holy Place mean for new covenant believers? As important, are there things that can hinder or enhance access to God in the new covenant? The next step in our journey takes us to the answers.

CHAPTER 5

A MODEL for DEVOTIONAL LIFE, PART 1

IT'S EASIER THAN we think to confuse the end with the means. I had invested twenty years of my life developing spiritual disciplines like reading through the Bible, memorizing Scripture verses, and daily meditation in Scripture. But in Russia I was finding that I could do all of that and still miss God and what he desires for me. I was doing all the "right stuff." But somehow in doing it I forgot that the purpose of these disciplines was not to build my case. You see, I wanted God to know why he should bless me — "I've done all of this to make you happy, so why won't you bless me?" I had confused the end with the means. The goal was not to do the disciplines well; the goal was to connect with God himself. On the hard gray brick of Red Square, I realized that I needed a way of relating to God that helped me keep him the goal and the disciplines the means I use to connect with him. I needed a whole devotional life, not just disconnected parts that didn't give me what I needed, especially in the desert.

Devotional life is a life of worship on a much different level than popular religion often foists on us. It is more than something we do before the pastor comes up to preach. It's not just a time of prayer and Scripture meditation before I begin my day, though these activities are important. Devotional life is more a lifestyle or a way of living. It is interesting that in the New Testament, the concept of worship extends far beyond the bounds of formal, organized worship services, right into the details of everyday life. The apostle Paul, for instance, says that we should present our bodies a living sacrifice to God and that this is our reasonable service of worship to God (Romans 12:1). In saying this, the apostle moves worship beyond the limits of formal religious activity into the realm of daily life.[1] To present our bodies a living sacrifice to God means that anything that our bodies can do, except sin, should be done as an act of worship to God. No area of human life, then, is excluded from worship, and no part of our human nature is excluded: body, soul, spirit, mind, will, and emotions.

Thus devotional life is a much more complete picture of worship than we are accustomed to. Devotional life is the true inner life of a person, not so much what we say as how we think, what we hope and long for, how we make decisions, what we really believe, what we doubt, and what we trust. The apostle Paul says in Philippians 2:12, "Work out your salvation with fear and trembling." Our devotional life is where we work out our salvation.[2]

Another aspect of devotional life is communion with God. Communion includes two big ideas: union and sharing. When we speak about communion with God, we are talking about a special and unique union that we have with God through Jesus Christ. Jesus says that when someone comes into a right relationship with him, both he and the Father come and make their dwelling with the person (John 14:23). One of the blessings of new covenant relationship is that God comes to dwell in us: Jesus dwells in our hearts by faith (Ephesians 3:17) and our very bodies become temples of the Holy Spirit who dwells in us (1 Corinthians 3:16; 6:19; Romans 8:9). This is the basis for a profound experience of God in our daily devotional life. We share in the life of God because he literally lives in us. But as Jesus taught in John 15 the branches must abide in the vine to receive their life and sustenance. Devotional life is the inner life of a person connected to the very presence of God himself to receive all he or she needs for life and wholeness.

But how does that connection happen? By what path can we connect to this source of life, especially when we are in a desert? It is the tabernacle that gives us a model for approaching God's very person. The tabernacle provides a model for the new covenant believer's devotional life. Let's take a look.

APPROACHING A GOD WHO IS HOLY

If we could jump into a helicopter and fly over the nation of Israel during the time it was camped in the desert, the sight would be fascinating. We would notice three circles of human life and activity: an outer, middle, and inner circle (see illustration 1 on page 56). The twelve tribes of Israel formed the outer circle. The tribes camped in order, three on each side—north, south, east, and west—forming the outer ring of the camp.[3] Inside of the tribes we would see a middle ring formed by the families of the Levites.[4] Last, the inner area was formed by the courtyard and its centerpiece, the tabernacle itself. And remember, during these days a pillar of cloud stood over the tabernacle by day and a column of fire by night (Exodus 40:34-38).

The clear message of this design is that the Lord is in the midst of his people. In the center of the camp God made himself visible in the cloud and fire over the tabernacle. But there is more. God designated the families of the Levites to take care of the tabernacle, and he set them apart especially for this task.[5] He also appointed them to camp immediately surrounding the tabernacle. This was not by accident. God was communicating to Israel that he is a holy God, and that human beings cannot approach him and live, except through the means of cleansing he provides. When we say God is holy, we mean that by his nature God is separate from all that is impure, sinful, and morally or otherwise imperfect. Because sin entered the world through Adam and Eve's disobedience, we are all warped by sin from the inside out.[6] This disqualifies us from access to a God who is holy. For someone to approach a God who by nature is pure perfection, he or she must be made holy by God

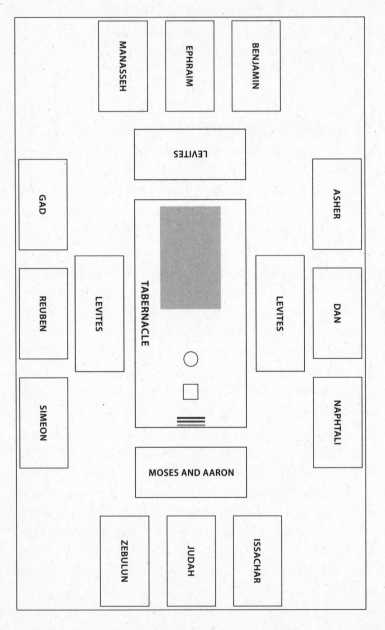

Illustration 1

and must approach God by a path of holiness that ensures he or she is ready to meet this God. In fact the Lord God is described as "holy, holy, holy."[7] To communicate the seriousness of this, God put the Levites around the tabernacle like insulation around a high-power wire.

Numbers 1:53 tells us that God commanded the Levites to camp around the tabernacle to keep the Israelites from straying into the tabernacle area. It was a place so holy that trespassers who were not authorized to enter would be put to death. The haunting phrase repeated in the book of Numbers is that "Anyone else who goes near it shall be put to death."[8]

God appointed the sons of Aaron to be priests, and they camped directly across from the entrance to the courtyard of the tabernacle. God made a distinction between the people of Israel and the Levites, and he made a distinction between the Levites and the priests. The priests were the ones who went into the tabernacle regularly to minister before God, as we will see shortly. It was the priests who were to prepare the ark of the covenant for transportation and to carry it—not the Levites, on penalty of death.[9] The Levites were also not allowed to touch the furnishings inside the tabernacle on penalty of death, but they were to carry them using poles that did not require them to make contact with the articles. So serious were these parts of the Law that if the Levites violated it and came near the furnishings of the tabernacle, the priests as well as the Levites were to be put to death (Numbers 18:3).

God was making a point. He is a holy God, and those who would approach him must do so on his terms, because his terms are the only terms that make us suitable to appear before him. Under the old covenant only the priests could enter the tabernacle to minister before God. One priest was chosen to serve as the high priest who represented the people before God and represented God to the people. This was especially true on the Day of Atonement, Yom Kippur, when he would take the blood of a bull and goat into the Holiest of All to cover the nation's sins for a year.[10] Even the high priest could enter the Holiest of All only on Yom Kippur, and at no other time.[11] The path to God's presence was closed to most Israelites, and even to the high priest himself, except once a year.

The only way an Israelite could become a priest was by birth into the family of Aaron.[12] God's original design was that the entire nation would be priests to serve before him.[13] The nation did not keep his covenant, so God limited the priesthood to the descendants of Aaron, the first high priest. It is interesting that one result of the sacrifice of Christ is that we who are followers of Christ are now made priests—as a matter of fact, we become a holy nation and a royal priesthood, as God originally intended with Israel.[14] So we become "priests" before God by being born again into the family of God by faith in Christ and can enter the Most Holy Place of his presence. The perfect sacrifice of Jesus, the superior High Priest, cleanses us as worshippers to an extent that we are now able to approach the very presence of God.[15] The One who is holy created a way for a people who are unholy by nature to approach him. As we move through the courtyard and the tabernacle we will see many furnishings and activities that foreshadow Jesus and his work. Let's look now at how the tabernacle makes that Way more understandable to us.

A PLACE OF SATISFACTION

The courtyard was the very center of the Israelite camp. Shimmering white curtains, seven and a half feet high, outlined the tabernacle area.[16] To enter the court we would pass through the entrance marked by a curtain of embroidered blue, scarlet, and purple yarn.[17] This was the only entrance to the court, and thus the path to God's presence had but one door. It's difficult to miss the parallel of this to Jesus Christ, whom the whole tabernacle and its offerings foreshadow. John records Jesus' own words declaring, "I am the gate; whoever enters through me will be saved. He will come in and go out, and find pasture" (John 10:9). The book of Hebrews declares that we have boldness to enter the Holiest of All through the new and living way Jesus opened by his sacrifice on the cross.[18] We may not enter the presence of God by just any way, but the way he provided in Jesus, who is the way, the truth, and the life.[19]

Once inside the courtyard, three prominent structures grab our attention: the bronze altar, the bronze laver, and the tabernacle. Worship in the old covenant centered around these three areas of the courtyard. For King David and other leaders of Israel, the courts of the Lord's house was the place they would go to find joy and deep satisfaction:

Enter into his gates with thanksgiving, and into his courts with praise: be thankful unto him, and bless his name. (Psalm 100:4, KJV)

Blessed is the man whom thou choosest, and causest to approach unto thee, that he may dwell in thy courts: we shall be satisfied with the goodness of thy house, even of thy holy temple. (Psalm 65:4, KJV)

The courtyard was satisfying because it was there that people were reconciled to God and restored to a right relationship with him. It was there that they would see visible manifestations of God's presence with them. It was there that people came to meet God Almighty and to hear what he had to say to them. And it was there that God chose to meet with them.

This is the image that hit me in Red Square! There was a place I could go that would give me a joy and satisfaction that transcended the limited effects of life's pain and disappointments. And there was a door, a gate to enter that place. The door is Jesus Christ; he is the door and the Way.[20] On that day in Moscow, bewildered and numb, I took a feeble but determined step to look to Jesus, the Way, the door who gives me entrance into the realm of reality where God can be experienced. Taking my lead from Psalm 100:4, I began to praise God for his Son, Jesus, and for all he did for me at such great cost and to ask him to help me take full advantage of the way he had opened into the very presence of God.

But what is it that's so satisfying about the courtyard of the tabernacle? Certainly I needed to seek satisfaction in the Lord. I should find my deepest joy in life in the One who created it, not in the praise I received from others. These were issues I needed to deal with, but something else deeper was gnawing at me. Then underneath all my questions and that feeling that I hadn't gotten to the bottom of it yet, I found something I didn't expect.

There was something else there, something primordial and intriguing about the courts of the tabernacle. It was the beauty of God! If anything would be satisfying, it would be basking in the beauty of the most perfect being in the universe. David said that one thing he would do in the sanctuary was "to behold the beauty of the LORD."[21] Because the tabernacle is the dwelling place of God, it is the place we can go to experience the beauty of God. Anyone can behold breathtaking mountain majesty or the astonishing beauty of the undersea world and still fall into the trap of worshipping the creation and miss the perfect beauty of the Creator.[22] It is the "Beauty" (capital "B") to which all natural beauty (lowercase "b") points, declaring God's glory.[23]

As we will see, the tabernacle was a place of great beauty. Fashioned out of pure gold and covered with fine linen curtains exquisitely embroidered in blue, scarlet, and purple, the tabernacle was a place of stunning beauty. So for the high priest to enter such a room, he also had to be made beautiful. In Exodus 28 God gives specific instructions for the garments of Aaron, the high priest. He says in verses 2 and 40 that these elaborate and striking garments are to give the high priest glory and beauty.[24] We have seen the importance of God's holiness in the structure of the camp and the courtyard.

David shows us that beauty is an aspect of God's holiness when he exhorts those who approach God to worship the Lord in the beauty of his holiness.[25] The garments made for Aaron's glory and beauty to enter the Holiest of All are described as *holy* garments. Beauty is an important quality of the holiness of God and his presence. So next we take the first steps into this beauty as we come into the courts of the Lord's house.

THE BRONZE ALTAR

Passing through the blue, scarlet, and purple curtain we come before a harsh scene. The roaring flames of a chest-high, square, bronze fire pit[26] confront us, and the smell of roasting meat is everywhere. We hear the moan of animals about to be slaughtered, and notice the blood of other animals splattered around the base of the altar. It is a brutal and messy sight. And this is the path to the presence of God? Yes.

The altar was a place of death. An Israelite would bring an animal from his flock or herd to a priest at the bronze altar. The Israelite would place his hand on the head of the animal, signifying the animal's taking upon itself the sin of the person, and the Israelite would slaughter the animal right there. The priest would then take the blood of the animal and sprinkle it on the sides of the altar, atoning[27] for the sin of the person. The animal was then cut into pieces and the pieces were burned to ashes on the altar.[28] The altar, then, served as a place of sacrifice[29] where animals were killed in place of people who were guilty of sin.

The altar has two levels of significance for us today. First, the altar and the sacrifices upon it are a powerful picture foreshadowing the perfect sacrifice of Jesus Christ. The entrance of sin into the world brought a horrible curse on every human being; the penalty for sin was death.[30] This is what was so humbling about the offerings at the bronze altar. A person had to bring one of his innocent animals to the altar, lay his hands on the head of the animal — transferring his guilt to the animal — and then kill the animal. Now that's a living parable to teach us the horror of sin in God's eyes.

Death is the only thing that God will accept to remove the penalty of sin and restore relationship with him. This is where Jesus steps into the world as the perfect sacrifice. The book of Hebrews compares the perfect sacrifice of Jesus to the imperfect sacrifices at the bronze altar, which could not take away sin.[31] The bronze altar points us to the perfect sacrifice of Jesus, which did not have to be offered every year, but only once.[32] And without a sacrifice that takes away sin there would be no chance to approach a God who is holy. Without the altar, there would be no way to remove sin; there would be no path to God's presence.

There is a second significance of the bronze altar for us: The parallel between the altar of the old covenant and the cross of the new covenant. Both were instruments of death and places of sacrifice. Both were places where a sacrifice for sin made it possible for a person who was guilty and separated from God because of sin to be reconciled to God. Before Jesus went to the cross he made this statement about those who would follow him: "If anyone would come after me, he must deny himself and take up his cross daily and follow me."[33]

Like the altar, the cross was an instrument of death. Jesus taught his followers that the way to life begins with death. Jesus himself showed us what this death of the cross means for us the night before he died. Jesus was in agony in the Garden of Gethsemane as he prayed, "Father, if you are willing, take this cup from me; yet not my will, but yours be done."[34] Jesus was facing death on a cross, the most brutal form of execution in his day. But he was also facing something he had never experienced in eternity: separation from the Father when he bore the sins of the world on his body as the perfect sacrifice. Jesus expressed to the Father the human feeling of his pain, and then he said something remarkable. After asking the Father if it were possible to avoid this horrible a death, he submitted his will to the will of the Father. The bronze altar and the cross are the places of sacrifice where we choose to die to self-will. Jesus said "not my will, but your will be done." At the altar, I must place my will and let it die so that the impulse of my heart might be to do the will of God.

Perhaps the greatest example of this in the Old Testament is the story of Abraham and Isaac. After waiting one hundred years for a son and watching that son grow for several years, Abraham was told by God to take his son to a mountain and offer him as a sacrifice to God. Can you imagine the conflict in Abraham's heart? He had waited over a hundred years for this, and now God wanted him to give it up. With his will broken and his soul in anguish, Abraham lifted the knife to kill his own son on an altar.[35] There, at the altar, Abraham submitted his will to God and expressed that submission in the act of raising the knife to kill his son, certainly not his will. Abraham sacrificed a ram in place of his son Isaac, but the real sacrifice had already taken place. That was the sacrifice of Abraham's will on the altar, humbling and submitting his will to God's.

In the summer of 1977, I attended a spiritual life conference for college students in Detroit. The theme of the conference was "Here am I, Lord, send me." The opening speaker began by saying that he was in his first year of medical school and the Lord had made it clear to him that he was to leave medicine and instead invest his life in the spiritual well-being of thousands of college students around the world. I sat in my seat listening to these words with two applications to medical school in my backpack. I had gone to Texas A&M University because of its premed program, was completing my final year of studies, and was looking forward to serving God as a physician. That was my will, what I wanted to do. There was nothing wrong with that; many of my friends followed God to medical school, and that's what I wanted to do.

For five long days I walked up and down the Detroit River wrestling with God, trying to offer him a "deal" that would allow me to do what I wanted and still make him happy. God was silent. He was waiting on me to place my "Isaac" on the altar. The problem was that my desire for medicine was occupying the place in my heart that God wanted. As the conference ended I laid my "Isaac" of medicine on the altar. Being the good Bible student that I was, I waited for the angel to come and grab the knife before it plunged into the desire of my heart. The angel never showed up, so I exchanged the operating room for dorm rooms and living rooms from Memphis to Moscow, where surgery didn't happen with the blade of a scalpel but with truth of Scripture.

It was not my will, but God's will I needed to trust, and this scene at the altar is one I've had to repeat many times over the years.

The bronze altar is the first piece of furniture we encounter on the path to the presence of God. Its message for us is clear: Unless we die to self-will we will move no closer to God than the altar. God reigns over the universe and he gives us a choice to follow him or not. The choice is ours; the journey begins or ends at the altar.

THE BRONZE LAVER

Moving beyond the bronze altar we come to another object of bronze, a basin filled with water resting on a pedestal. The bronze basin, or laver, is the place where priests washed themselves before entering the tabernacle to perform their priestly duties.[36] In fact the priests are warned in Exodus 30:20-21 that they are to wash their hands and feet, not only for the practical result of having clean hands and feet but also for the symbolic power of cleansing themselves before coming into the presence of a holy God. Every priest who came into the tabernacle had to cleanse himself or face possible death for attempting to enter God's presence inappropriately.

In the book of Hebrews we see the new covenant reality to which the bronze laver points. The laver speaks of cleansing, but the extent of the cleansing in the new covenant is of a whole new order with an amazing new result. Hebrews 9:6-10 reminds us that only the high priest could enter the Holiest of All, and even then he could do it only once a year on Yom Kippur. The author of Hebrews goes on to call the first tabernacle a "parable"[37] for the time of the old covenant in which the path into the Holiest of All was severely restricted. Why is the path restricted? The author of Hebrews explains that next. He says that the old covenant sacrifices cleansed the believers in only an external and ceremonial sense, but did not purify them in a substantive, transformational way. The sacrifices of the old covenant did not cleanse down to the very conscience of the worshipper. This type of "imperfect" cleansing did not adequately purify a person to enter into the Holiest of All.[38] When Christ came and died on the cross, he opened a new way into the Holiest of All precisely because his sacrifice was perfect, namely the body of the one and only Son of God who lived a perfect life.[39]

This level of cleansing has new significance for those of us who are in Jesus Christ. As we pointed out in chapter 3, the problem with the first covenant was that the heart of the people constantly went astray from God,[40] and in fact, the prophet Jeremiah, who records the new covenant, also says that sin was engraved on the hearts of Israel with an engraving pen. He concludes that their hearts were deceitful above everything and wicked.[41] Remember that Jeremiah's prophecy tells us that in the new covenant the law is not written on external tables of stone, but internally on our hearts.[42] The cleansing of the conscience is real because God has given us a new heart. There is substance behind our cleansed consciences: We have received a new heart in Christ.

Hebrews tells us that this new heart is cleansed from a guilty conscience so that we are able to draw near to God.[43] Guilt is that nagging voice we can't turn off. It feels like a fifty-pound suitcase of rocks we carry to the store, around the house, and to work. We wonder why we're so tired all the time. Guilt weighs us down and shapes how we think, how we relate to others. The cleansing that Jesus offers takes away the guilt of the sins we commit against others, but it also removes the effects of the sins others commit against us.[44] One dangerous effect of the pain we feel when others sin against us is shame. Shame doesn't say *I did* something wrong, shame says *I am* something wrong.

Shame will define us if its power is not broken. The sacrifice of Jesus does not only deal with the guilt of our sin but also the shame of our sin. He clothes us with his righteousness and doesn't leave us in the nakedness of our own shame.[45] Instead of being paralyzed by the memory and pain of shameful things we have done or that were done to us, we can come boldly into God's presence because he has put a robe of beauty around us, the robe of his righteousness. We don't have to hang our heads in shame; we can humble ourselves before God and receive cleansing from the guilt and shame of sin through the sacrifice of Jesus. This new level of cleansing will enable us to step into the presence of the eternal King of the universe.

As the crackling heat of the bronze altar reminds us of the sacrifice of Christ and of our self-will, and the purifying waters of the bronze laver point us to the cleansing of our innermost being, we gaze upon the mystery of the tabernacle. The ornate curtain in front of us covers the entrance to the tabernacle and stirs our intrigue for what lies beyond. We find confidence to enter this place of deep satisfaction and unimaginable beauty because of the new way Jesus opened for us through his sacrifice. The bronze altar and laver have brought us through a process of confession, cleansing, and submission, and now we are ready to step within the tabernacle.

CHAPTER 6

A MODEL for DEVOTIONAL LIFE, PART 2

IT WASN'T HARD to figure out what was at the center of the Israelite camp. From miles around passersby would pause and wonder at this astonishing sight—a pillar of cloud and fire descending from the sky upon a curious-looking tent structure.[1] The tent looked plain enough except for the blinding brilliance of its gold pillars in the early morning light. In the middle of the desert, a dry and desolate wasteland, stood this tent about the size of a trailer home,[2] just like the trailer where I lived in Tuskegee.

During those early years in Tuskegee, God caught my attention with the beauty and power of the tabernacle as a model for my devotional life. I was alone and losing courage for the very work that inspired my move to the Deep South. I remember returning home one hot Alabama night, discouraged and lonely. As I walked up to the trailer under the glistening moonlight, it hit me: I was not alone. This was more than a feeling. My trailer was becoming my tabernacle. It was where I lived out and worked out my relationship with God. It was where I cried out to God for mercy and understanding; it was where I awoke after midnight in anguish of heart, mulling over the news from home—one more of my childhood friends graduated from medical school. And although I had obeyed God, I felt left behind, in a maze of uncertainty. It was there I realized that the key for my life lay in the realities to which the tabernacle pointed me. I had to step into the way of the tabernacle and follow its path into the very presence of God to find what he had for me.

THE HOLY PLACE

Blue, scarlet, and purple curtains hung between five golden pillars to mark the entrance to the tabernacle.[3] This no doubt intrigued the worshippers who could not enter the room behind it. The curtain formed a boundary only the priests could pass as they went to minister within the tabernacle. The earthy bronze of the furnishings in the courtyard gave place to the shimmering gold of the tabernacle interior. The inner space of the tabernacle was divided into two parts: an outer room, the Holy Place, and an inner room, the Holiest of All.[4] These titles for the rooms of the tabernacle again call our attention to the holiness of God and remind us that we human beings are not fit to enter the presence of God on the basis of our own merits. It is only God who can outfit us with the righteousness and holiness[5] necessary to enter his presence as we come to him through his Son, Jesus, the High Priest of the new covenant. In this gold-laden room the noise, glare, and aroma of the world gave way to a more sublime stillness, one that pointed to heaven itself.

As the curtain closed behind them, the priests faced a small golden altar with a richly embroidered veil behind it. On the left was a golden candlestick and on the right a golden table with loaves of bread (see illustration 2 on page 69). With the glare of natural light shut out by the veil, the light of the candlestick reflected off the gold and the rich colors of the interior wall hangings to produce an ethereal hue that let the priests know they were in a very different place. As we have seen, the sanctuary represents the dwelling place of God in heaven. So when the priests entered the Holy Place they were entering a model of heaven itself where God dwells.[6] But there was more. The priests were also showing us the path to experiencing God's presence on earth.

Illustration 2

THE TABERNACLE AND ITS FURNITURE

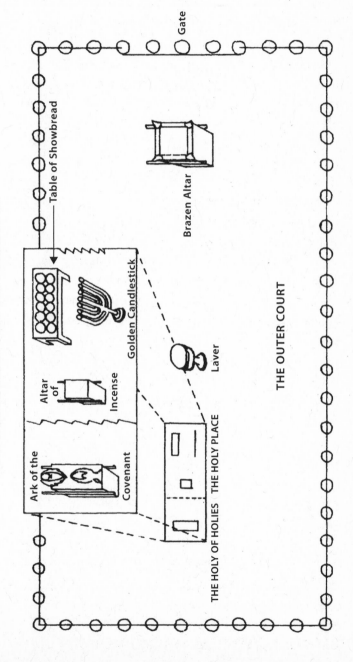

HOW TO USE A MODEL

Before we delve into the significance of the Holy Place, we need to think about what a model is and isn't, and how we use it. In elementary school, I loved making models of fighter jets. When I placed the canopy on my plastic version of the F-4 Phantom, my eyes were fixed on this scale model of a real fighter jet. But the model was not the real thing. As I gazed at this replica of the fighter, I didn't imagine myself sitting in an oversized piece of plastic making airplane noises with my mouth. I dreamed of roaring off the deck of an aircraft carrier in a supersonic fighter jet and doing barrel rolls as I accelerated skyward and watched the huge aircraft carrier beneath me become a postage stamp floating on the ocean. That's what a model does! A model ignites our imagination and helps us understand reality and possibility. As breathtaking as I'm sure it would be to watch the horizon go round and round while my jet performed an aerobatic maneuver, it pales in comparison with stepping beyond the veil into the presence of the God who created motion and all the laws of physics that make flight possible. Now let's look at the model of the tabernacle.

THE GOLDEN CANDLESTICK

On the south side of the Holy Place stood the ornate seven-branched golden candlestick.[7] Each of the seven branches contained a lamp or small bowl atop it containing olive oil, which was the fuel of the candlestick. The priests lit the lamps in the evenings and extinguished them in the mornings when they cleaned and refilled them.[8] The candlestick was the only source of light in the tabernacle.

While light may be used to refer to many things in Scripture,[9] we will focus on a couple that are relevant to the candlestick. First, light refers to God himself. Second Samuel 22:29 says, "You are my lamp, O LORD; the LORD turns my darkness into light." God meets us in the midst of confusion, disorientation, and discouragement and turns our darkness into light. This is a description of God meeting us in the desert!

The desert is often a place of darkness. In the dark we cannot see, and what we cannot see can hurt us. God is the Light that illuminates the ground in front of us so that we can see where to go. The priests needed the light of the golden candlestick to do their work, and we need the light of God for our life journey.

When David's spirit was downcast he asked God to send his light and his truth to guide him. The light led David to God himself. This was significant because God was David's joy and delight.[10] It is in the light of God's presence that we find real joy and delight, and this joy and delight is not based on circumstances, but on an unchanging God whose love is perfect. The light of the golden candlestick points us to God himself, the source of light, and to Jesus, his Son, the Light of the World.[11] Jesus revealed the Father in a way that no previous form of revelation had ever done.[12] He is the express image of God, and he alone was at the Father's side and is able to reveal him.[13]

In my early weeks in Tuskegee, I often returned home downcast after a hard day on campus. Another day of fruitless effort against what felt like an immovable wall of opposition. After a little something to eat, I would head out behind my trailer where a small patch of grass on the red earth awaited me. I knelt before God under the moonlit sky and felt the golden glow of the candlestick pointing me to God and his Son, Jesus, the true Light. I knew that there, in his presence, I would find the joy and delight to fuel my faith, sustain my hope, and fill me with the love that would make everything right.

The light of the golden candlestick also points us to the way God reveals himself through His Word and His Spirit. Throughout the Old Testament—from the prophet Samuel[14] to the Psalms[15] and the Major and Minor Prophets[16]—we find God revealing himself through his Word. The Scripture is referred to as a "lamp" and a "light" to show us the way of life.[17] God's Word gives us wisdom to live every aspect of life in a manner that pleases him and connects to his life and power.[18] In the New Testament the Word of God is not only written, but alive in the person of the Son of God.[19] Jesus makes it clear that one of his most important jobs on earth is to reveal the Father.[20] The New Testament also helps us to see that it is the Spirit of God who enlightens our understanding so that we can grasp the knowledge of God through his written Word.[21]

The quietness of the Holy Place with the flicker of the golden candlestick invites us to the one source of true light and life, to God himself. Just as the light of the candlestick illuminates the outer chamber of the tabernacle, the light of God's revelation in his Son and by his Word and his Spirit illuminates our hearts and minds, making it possible for us to attain a deeper knowledge of God.

THE GOLDEN TABLE OF SHOWBREAD

Directly across the room from the golden candlestick was a golden table just above knee-height with twelve loaves of bread on it.[22] The loaves, which were set out fresh each Sabbath,[23] were placed in two rows of six, with some incense along each row.[24] The bread, called showbread, was to be eaten only by the priests, and it had to be eaten in a holy place because it was considered to be one of the most holy substances in the tabernacle.[25]

The bread of the golden table provided food for the priests. This element of the tabernacle speaks of the importance of spiritual nourishment in our devotional life. While this is true of life in general, it is a matter of life and death in the desert. In Deuteronomy 8, Moses reminded the children of Israel that God used their desperate hunger in the desert to teach them that people don't live by bread alone, but by every word that proceeds out of the mouth of the Lord.[26] During his forty days in the desert, Jesus recalled this passage and quoted it to the Devil when he tempted him. Jesus refers to the Word of God as "bread" for our spiritual life. For bread to be of value to us we have to eat it. That means we have to chew and swallow it, then let the process of digestion do its work for the bread to help us. When I eat a piece of bread, the same morsel that was in my mouth an hour ago is now broken down into its elemental parts and is ready to become part of my body.

So it is with our devotional life. Before the process of spiritual digestion can begin, we have to open our mouths spiritually and take in God's Word by hearing or reading. Sadly, we all too often stop here. The real process of digestion starts when we do what Scripture calls meditation. In meditation we "chew" the Word and break it down to get out of it the spiritual nourishment we need to fuel our lives. This is where we need the light of the Holy Spirit to illuminate our understanding; he helps us draw the nourishment from the Word of God. But then it's up to us; we have to submit ourselves to what we find in God's Word and apply it. We can chew on the Word by meditation and study, but until we submit to it, we will never get it into our system. The goal is for the bread of God's Word to become part of our spiritual life as we submit to it and apply it over time.

One day I was reflecting on Isaiah 41:10, "So do not fear, for I am with you; do not be dismayed, for I am your God. I will strengthen you and help you; I will uphold you with my righteous right hand." I was preparing to lead a historic gathering of 120 top leaders from all parts of The U.S. Navigators. They were coming to New York City for an immersion experience in ethnic diversity and to consider how we might grow into a more ethnically diverse organization that better represents God's kingdom.

As I faced the sheer size of this responsibility, I could feel my fear rising and my confidence falling. It was then that I entered the "Holy Place" and took the "bread" of Isaiah 41:10 and began to chew on it before God. I began to notice that God had promised to be with me, to be my God, to strengthen me, to help me, and to uphold me with his strong right arm. I saw that my part was to not fear or be dismayed. As I reflected on these realities over several days, my fear gave way to a quiet confidence that was rooted in the Word of God. So with a deep sense of my inadequacy and God's power, I stepped into this event, and the result? The Navigators is a different organization today as a result of our days in New York. His Word gave strength to my inner life as I meditated on it, submitted to it, and applied it. The golden table of showbread invites us to a regular diet of God's Word to sustain our spiritual lives.

THE ALTAR OF INCENSE

Before the inner veil stood a waist-high golden altar.[27] It was square and had horns atop its four corners,[28] and two golden rings that held the golden poles used to transport it.[29] This was not like the bronze altar; no sacrifices were burned on it. This altar was for burning sweet incense, which produced a cloud of smoke with a uniquely pleasing aroma.[30] The priests would take coals from the bronze altar and bring them into the Holy Place in a metal container (censer) and place them on the golden altar. Then they would put sweet incense on the coals, filling the tabernacle with a fragrant aroma. The priests would do this twice a day: when the golden candlestick was lit in the evening and when it was extinguished in the morning.[31]

The golden altar served another important purpose. On the Day of Atonement, the high priest sprinkled blood on the horns of the golden altar as part of the process of atoning for the sins of the people for the year.[32] Thus, this altar was considered most holy to the Lord. The penalties for violating it, for being careless with the ritual—including the use of incense—were grave, as we see in the death of two of Aaron's sons.[33] Here again we find a sobering reminder of the holiness of God; we may approach God, but on his terms, not ours.

The altar of incense points us to the place of prayer in approaching God's presence. Psalm 141:2 says, "May my prayer be set before you like incense; may the lifting up of my hands be like the evening sacrifice." In Scripture incense, and especially the cloud of incense coming from the altar, is a picture of our prayer before God. In the book of Revelation the apostle John paints a scene of heaven where the true golden altar of incense is visible.[34] This altar is the heavenly reality to which the golden altar points. In this vision the prayers of the saints are offered like incense to God, a sweet aroma pleasing to him.[35] Our prayers can become the aroma around God's heavenly throne. The most compelling image of incense from the golden altar comes next and gives us a life-changing insight into how prayer can connect us with God. For this we must go into the Holiest of All.

THE THRONE ROOM OF GOD

Passing the dance of amber light on the pillars of gold and the brush of rich blue, scarlet, and purple linen we come into the most unique fifteen-foot square of space on the earth.[36] Through the inner curtain was the one place on the planet where God would meet with humanity regularly year after year. It was there that God chose to make his dwelling among his people. This curtain, or veil, separated the Holy Place from the Holiest of All. It was a significant barrier to experiencing God's presence because only the high priest could go beyond the veil, and he could do it only once a year.[37] The way into God's presence was limited to a single day of the year and to a single person out of the entire nation.

The only piece of furniture in the Holiest of All was the ark of the covenant. This rectangular chest made of acacia wood was overlaid inside and out with pure gold and had four golden rings for the golden poles used to carry it.[38] God commanded Moses to place three articles inside the ark: a golden pot containing manna, Aaron's rod that sprouted buds, and the stone tablets of the Law Moses received on Mount Sinai.[39]

The pot of manna reminded the people of God's amazing provision for them in the desert. He wanted his people to remember that he fed them with bread from heaven when they had nothing to eat. When God leads his people into the desert, he feeds them and often sustains them in a manner they cannot explain in human terms. Remember, the word *manna* in Hebrew means, "What is it?"[40] The Hebrews had no idea what this miraculous food was, but they knew God provided it for them in the desert. In John 6 Jesus draws a distinct parallel between himself and the manna of the desert: "I am the bread of life. Your forefathers ate the manna in the desert, yet they died. But here is the bread that comes down from heaven, which a man may eat and not die. I am the living bread that came down from heaven."[41] Jesus was saying that he himself was the bread that came from heaven to give true life to people, the life of heaven, eternal life. Jesus was offering himself as the bread from heaven that we could eat and live forever. The light of New Testament revelation in Jesus shines back on the golden pot of manna to show us that manna in the desert was a picture of what God was to provide in Jesus. Those who ate the bread in the desert died, but those who come to Jesus and take him into their lives by faith will have a new quality of life, a life that doesn't end.[42]

In this world Jesus Christ is the only spiritual nourishment that sustains us with a life that transcends this world. He connects us with a very different world, where God dwells in heaven. And as we by faith take in Jesus, the bread of life, he comes to live in our hearts.[43] In the desert it is Jesus himself who nourishes us. There is nothing else to eat that satisfies and sustains us in the wasteland of the desert. At the center of God's presence — in the ark of the covenant — was the golden pot of manna, a vivid reminder that God nourishes and nurtures his people in the desert. God invites us to a banquet table where he himself is the main course. Have we yet learned what it means when Jesus says, "I am the bread of life. He who comes to me will never go hungry, and he who believes in me will never be thirsty" (John 6:35)? This is not just a metaphor; it's intended to be our experience in Jesus Christ. The most complete satisfaction we can get in life is in God himself.

Numbers 17 tells the story of the Levites' objection to God's decision to limit the priestly duties to Aaron and his sons.[44] God expressed his displeasure with these men harshly by putting to death 250 of them. Then to further confirm his decree for the old covenant priesthood, he had each of the twelve tribes place a wooden staff before the ark of the covenant. The following morning the only staff that had budded and sprouted almonds was Aaron's; this was the sign God said would accompany his favor. God commanded Moses to place Aaron's staff in front of the ark of the covenant as a sign for those who rebelled against God.[45] Aaron's staff, the only one that budded, was the second object placed in the ark.

The ark of the covenant contained the most powerful symbols in the old covenant faith. The golden pot of manna reminded Israel of God's covenant provision for them, even in the deserts of life. Aaron's rod reminded Israel of God's holiness and that he had set apart only one family to serve close to him as priests, and that was the family of Aaron. God did not respect the Levites' complaint, but affirmed his will for the priesthood to be limited to the descendants of Aaron, and confirmed it by making Aaron's staff grow almonds and flowers. To approach the Holy Place of the tabernacle in worship in the old covenant a person had to be a priest, and a person could only become a priest by birth into Aaron's family.

Because of the disobedience of Israel, the priesthood of the old covenant was limited to Aaron's descendants.[46] When Christ, the High Priest of the new covenant, arrived, he opened a completely new way to God, which did not require a system of sacrifices every year or birth into a certain human family. The new and living way invites us to place our trust and hope in the perfect sacrifice of Jesus, and by our faith in him we become members of God's family. Now, being his sons and daughters, we can come into the inner sanctuary of our heavenly Abba, Father.[47] Aaron's rod that budded points to the intimate access that God grants us into his unapproachable holy presence by the new way opened through his Son, Jesus.

On Mount Sinai, God gave Moses two tables of stone that contained the Ten Commandments written with the finger of God.[48] He commanded Moses to place these words of the Law in the ark of the covenant. The Law was a central part of the old covenant. It instructed God's people how to live, eat, govern themselves, handle infectious diseases, dispense justice in disputes, and a host of other things, including how to relate to him and maintain their relationship with him. The

Law contained his will for their lives under the old covenant, and it was referred to as the testimony, because it bore witness to the people of God's expectations of them in relationship with him.[49] Of the three objects in the ark, the Law was the one that was most enduring; by the time of Solomon's reign only the two stone tablets were in the ark.[50]

In the new covenant the Law is written on the tablets of our human heart (not on tablets of stone), which transforms our inner person, giving us a new heart.[51] This is what God does to outfit us for a new relationship with him. But we have a part also. Throughout the Old Testament God exhorted Israel to place his Law or his Word in their hearts. Consider these passages, for example:

> These commandments that I give you today are to be upon your hearts. (Deuteronomy 6:6)

> Do not let this Book of the Law depart from your mouth; meditate on it day and night, so that you may be careful to do everything written in it. Then you will be prosperous and successful. (Joshua 1:8)

> But his delight is in the law of the Lord, and on his law he meditates day and night. (Psalm 1:2)

> I have hidden your word in my heart that I might not sin against you. (Psalm 119:11)

God's Law was placed in the ark of the covenant because it contained the terms and conditions of God's relationship with his people and instructions for how they were to live. The Law in the ark of the covenant points us, in the new covenant, to the role of God's Word in our devotional life. Scripture records the mystery and character of our relationship with God in Jesus Christ. It is by meditating on God's Word day and night that we will begin to grasp the true nature of our relationship with the Father, Son, and Spirit, and in fact to know them.

The ark of the covenant stood just over two feet high[52] and was open at the top. A special removable lid was made to cover the ark. It was called the mercy seat, but it was no ordinary lid. The mercy seat was made of pure gold and was overshadowed by two figures mounted on each end. The figures were those of cherubim with their wings extended toward one another looking down over the ark.[53] The mercy seat was a place of atonement, where the high priest entered with the blood of animals to cover the sins of Israel for a year.[54] With its winged cherubim, the mercy seat was also the earthly representation of God's invisible throne in heaven. In Scripture cherubim are described as attendants of the throne of God.[55] The mercy seat crowned the ark of the covenant as God's representative throne on earth. The Holiest of All was the most holy place in the tabernacle because it was the very throne room of God in the world. The tabernacle was the dwelling place of God, and the ark of the covenant with its mercy seat was the place where God's presence dwelt, his throne. Exodus 25:22 says, "There, above the cover [mercy seat] between the two cherubim that are over the ark of the Testimony, I will meet with you and give you all my commands for the Israelites."[56]

The mercy seat above the ark is a model of the place where God meets with his people, at his throne. Let's look a bit more closely at the ark and mercy seat to understand how they can serve as a model for our devotional life. On the Day of Atonement, the Scriptures say that God met with the high priest in a cloud over the mercy seat.[57] It also tells us that the high priest was to take a container full of hot coals and put some incense on it so that the cloud of incense would cover the mercy seat; that way, the high priest wouldn't die.[58]

While experiencing God's presence in our lives certainly cannot be reduced to formulas, Scripture does give us examples of spiritual practices that can move us along the path into God's presence. One of those practices is praise. We have seen that incense is a figure for prayer.[59] Praise is one of the most powerful forms of prayer. Praise focuses our attention, not on what we can get from God, but on God himself who can give us anything. Praise is a type of prayer that focuses on the character and works of God. We praise God when we express to him our sense of awe and wonder at his mercy, love, goodness, justice, and glory. Or we praise him because of something he has done in creation, in Jesus Christ, or in our lives.

Praise, especially in the Old Testament, is not just a mental activity; it engages our emotions, our entire inner life, and our bodies. David says, "I will praise God with my whole heart."[60] The heart can be expressed to God in praise through song, painting, sculpture, dance, written word, spoken word, and certainly in other ways. Psalm 22:3 says that God is enthroned upon or dwells in the praises of his people. God was present in the incense above the mercy seat, and he is present in the "incense cloud" of our prayer and praise in daily life when we praise him. The author of Hebrews uses the imagery of offerings to portray our praise: "Through Jesus, therefore, let us continually offer to God a sacrifice of praise—the fruit of lips that confess his name."[61] Our praise is an offering to God, a sweet aroma of incense that fills the space around us and creates an environment that better enables us to connect with the God who is always there. God is omnipresent; he is everywhere. But because he is everywhere does not mean that we will experience him.

In earlier days television was broadcast by transmitting TV waves through the air. When I was growing up we loved to watch the show *Star Trek*, so we gathered every week in the family room to marvel at these adventures of space travel. But there was a problem as long as we didn't turn the TV set on—we didn't see anything. I could complain to the network that I couldn't see the show because I was busy talking and didn't have time to turn on the TV, but that was my problem. As soon as I made time to turn on the TV set, I could see the show in living color. That's how praise can work for us. Even though God's presence is everywhere, I can go through life disconnected from God, with my spiritual TV set turned off. Praise allows me to turn on my spiritual senses, tune in to the frequency of God's presence, and taste the goodness of his grace wherever I am.

INTO HIS PRESENCE

The ark of the covenant with its winged mercy seat was the crowning symbol of God's presence and power with his people in their camp, in travel, and in battle.[62] The ark brought the glory of God tangibly into the midst of his people,[63] and it was over the ark of the covenant that God met with a representative of the people in a cloud of incense. This is the imagery God chose to use to portray his new covenant relationship with believers.[64] The author of the book of Hebrews exhorts us to come boldly before God's throne of grace.[65] Then, after quoting Jeremiah's new covenant prophecy, he uses the tabernacle imagery he has developed to admonish his readers to enter the Holiest of All and draw near to God.[66]

In the tabernacle, God has given us a model for our devotional life in the new covenant. In chapter 5 we described our devotional life as a life of worship that engages our whole inner person and fills every aspect of our daily lives. Using this model of drawing near to God, we can enter the path to God's presence with praise and thanksgiving and pass into his courts at any time, and in any place.[67] I can do business with God at the bronze altar of sacrifice as I walk back to my desk from the water fountain and am tempted to lust or be prideful. Right then and there I can place my will and desire on the altar so it can die and set me free to do the will of the God I love.

At the bronze laver, I can allow the healing waters of God's grace in Christ to wash over the guilt and shame that condemn and confine me. Passing from natural light into the light of God's presence, I can come before the golden lampstand for the light of his Word to search me and give me wisdom for the day and the issues I face. I turn to the golden table of showbread to review a verse of Scripture I've memorized or meditate on a passage and receive strength and wisdom I can apply in word and in deed. I then look at the golden altar to recall that God looks at my prayer like sweet incense. Instead of a cloud of complaint limiting me, an aroma of praise can lift me to a new altitude that changes my perspective of life around me. Then I follow the words of Hebrews and enter the very throne room of God, the Holiest of All, and bask in the beauty of God's presence as I wait quietly for what he has to say.[68]

Devotional life embraces every area of life as a place I can experience God and worship him.[69] Our life of worship includes acts of service and the work we do in everyday life. We are to present our work and service to the Lord just as the priests offered their sacrifices to God,[70] and this means our financial giving also.[71] Devotional life means nurturing the habit of drawing near to God.[72] It may be a brief moment on a walk, a break at work, or a longer time early in the morning. Occasionally it can be a day or more alone with God in personal retreat. When we consider our lives over a longer period of time, like a year, we will want to have many different expressions of drawing near to God, from moments with him to minutes to hours to days. We draw near to God individually, but we also draw near to God in community with others. When we neglect worship in community we miss much of what God has for us, a subject we will take up in detail in chapter 12.[73]

Because the tabernacle is a model, it's important to remember that a model is not the real thing. A model doesn't work like a formula that promises if you do this then God will do that. It's more like a treasure map than a road map. The wise professor in *The Lion, the Witch and the Wardrobe* says to Lucy, "You won't get into Narnia again by *that* route."[74] We won't come into the experience of God's presence the same way every time. God is not predictable, but he is reliable. We don't want to slip into placing our confidence in a model, as God's people placed their confidence in the temple instead of the God who inhabited it.[75] The model is useful, but the object is God himself.

As a living picture of our devotional life, the tabernacle illuminates six paths to maturity, depth, and satisfaction in our relationship with God: knowing God, seeking God, hope, salvation, community, and mission. Our first journey is down the path of knowing God.

CHAPTER 7

"SISTER JONES KNOWS the SHEPHERD"

DESERTS REVEAL A lot about how deeply we know God. I was starting to feel comfortable. Getting around Moscow was fun. I enjoyed traveling and helping others travel around the country. On top of that I had some new Russian friends. I was starting to soar when the bottom fell out, and it wasn't pretty. Then in a puddle of dismay I realized God was testing my knowledge of him and my trust in him.

What does it mean to know God? Looking at the Old Testament we discover that knowing God is more than simply learning information about God. The Old Testament Hebrew word used most often for *know* is יָדַע (yaw·dah).[1] In the Old Covenant we find that this word speaks often of becoming acquainted with a person through relationship and personal experience.[2] The ideas of relationship and experience are so central to the word *yaw·dah* that it can even mean knowing someone through sexual intimacy.[3]

In the Hebrew world, knowing God was not merely knowing details about God, though this was also important. What was crucial was that a person knew God in relationship and experience. The psalmist declared, "O taste and see that the LORD is good."[4] This was not just an idea to be understood, it was something about God to experience. In several languages we find at least two kinds of words for the idea of "knowing." In Spanish, for example, the word *saber* means to know in the sense of awareness and understanding of details about things or people. The word *conocer*, however, means to know someone in relationship. God does not want his people to just collect information about him, he wants them to nurture a deep and abiding relationship with him.[5]

In the New Testament we find much the same idea, which is not a surprise because Jesus came from a Jewish background, as did Paul and most of the New Testament authors. From the very mouth of Jesus came these words: "Now this is eternal life: that they may know you, the only true God, and Jesus Christ, whom you have sent."[6] Eternal life itself is the journey of coming to know and enjoy an eternal and infinitely beautiful God. The apostle Paul enlightens our understanding of what it means to know God when he says, "I want to know Christ and the power of his resurrection and the fellowship of sharing in his sufferings, becoming like him in his death."[7] For Paul, to know Christ was not only to have access to the power of his resurrection but also to experience the sufferings of Christ.[8] Paul was a biblical scholar of his day, yet he didn't understand knowing Christ as a mere task of study but also as a journey of relating to him in worship, prayer, and obedience that led to experiencing his presence and power in life.

I am reminded of a story I heard during my days at Tuskegee. I went to visit a Tuskegee student who lived three hours from campus. In this little rural Alabama village stood an old wooden church building. When we gathered there to worship on Sunday, the whole building shook with the rhythmic foot patting of God's people singing Negro spirituals one after another. I heard that one day a distinguished young man came home from the university after completing his degree. Proud of this "local son" who had made it, he was asked to read the Twenty-Third Psalm. With eloquence and clarity this young man began to read, "The Lord is my shepherd I shall not want." Everyone was impressed and proud of this young man and his rendering of the famous psalm.

Sometime later it was time again to read Psalm 23. This time the congregation turned to one of its oldest members, known to everyone as "Sister Jones." Making her way to the front, Sister Jones rested her elbow on the lectern as she carefully turned the tattered pages of her Bible to the psalm. Then with a piercing gaze she said, "The Lawd is my Sheppad, I shaaall not want." When Sister Jones finished reading the psalm the church was in uproar with people standing, shouting, and waving handkerchiefs in the air. After the service a young man asked a deacon, "Now what's the difference between Sister Jones and the young man who read the same psalm a while ago?" The wise elderly man said, "Son, the young man knows the Twenty-Third Psalm; Sister Jones knows the Shepherd." Knowing God is an invitation to know the Shepherd.

Now Sister Jones had spent years hearing, reading, studying, memorizing, and meditating in the Scripture. What made the difference is what Sister Jones did with the ideas about God she learned by Bible reading, meditation, and the like. Scripture often speaks of the knowledge of God, not as the information we collect about God, but what results from our ideas about God colliding with reality.[9] Remember that in Deuteronomy 8:3 God says that he humbled his people and allowed them to hunger to help them to know him. What was God doing? Just like the clay and the potter, God was working on their knowledge of him like an unfinished lump of clay on a potter's wheel. God used the discipline of the desert like the work of a potter, carving away their wrong thinking about him and adding right thinking about him as he reshaped and molded their knowledge of him. Until my ideas about God are tested in the fire of reality they are just that, ideas. I must reflect on Scripture and study it to know God. But I should also realize that true knowledge of God is forged when my ideas about God collide with reality on the potter's wheel of life where God, the Sovereign Lord, is at work on the clay of my life.[10]

So knowing God is not simply collecting information about God. It is taking my ideas about God into the laboratory of life, and worship is one of the primary ways we do that. I'm speaking about worship understood in the holistic way the New Testament presents it.[11] This holistic way of worship we call "devotional life," and it enables us to connect with the living God in every part of our lives from what we feel like when we wake up in the morning to our last waking thought at night. Devotional life helps us connect with God in the heat of the desert when things don't make sense. When my life is a scrambled mess on the potter's wheel, there's somewhere I can go to meet the Potter himself. Worshipping God takes us down a path to meet with God, in a place where we can know him.

A PATH FOR KNOWING GOD

In chapter 5, we saw that the idea of worship in the New Testament has been expanded. The New Testament authors break worship out of the confines of the tabernacle courtyard and the temple precincts and bring it right into the grit and routine of daily life. Let's not discard the Old Testament, though, because it prepares us for this more holistic picture of devotional life with the imagery of the Old Testament sanctuary. Old and New Testament authors use language based on the model of the sanctuary to instruct God's people in the journey of knowing him.

The tabernacle was portable. During the years of Israel's wanderings in the desert, the tabernacle moved with them each time they broke camp.[12] God was ever present in the midst of his people. When they camped, the fire by night and cloud by day were visible signs of his presence in their midst. When they set out, the ark of the covenant symbolized the very throne of God accompanying Israel in travel and in battle.[13] We find an interesting parallel to this in the New Testament. The "mobile" sanctuary of the new covenant is the very body of those who belong to Jesus Christ. Paul says, "Do you not know that your body is a temple of the Holy Spirit, who is in you, whom you have received from God? You are not your own."[14] The presence of God in the midst of his people corporately in the Old Testament was a shadow of the superior indwelling of God in his people individually in the

New Testament.[15] Because our bodies are sanctuaries of God's Holy Spirit, we may come to God in any place because we are portable tabernacles of God's presence. This creates the opportunity for us to cultivate the discipline of practicing the presence of God.

God is present everywhere, but he is present in a unique way in the bodies of his people. Thus anywhere and at any time I can extend myself to God in a simple act faith and worship him. A seventeenth-century French monk known as Brother Lawrence explained this discipline when he declared that in the busiest time of dish washing he experienced God's presence with the same intense pleasure and reality as when he was alone in silent meditation. The whole of life is the context of knowing God, and often God will make himself known to us through events in our lives, just as he did with Israel.[16] In times of testing we experience God in new ways, and our knowledge of him grows. God invites us to practice the discipline of connecting with him right where we are. Whether you are in your car, on a bus, out walking, or on the job—whether you are at home, work, or play—choose to connect with him and know him right where you are.

And just how do we connect with God? Psalm 100:4 says to enter his gates with thanksgiving and his courts with praise. Wherever I am I can offer thanksgiving and praise to God. This is certainly one application of the apostle Paul's exhortation, "Pray without ceasing."[17] When we praise and thank God, our prayers create a cloud of incense, which comes before God's throne in heaven[18] where we can experience God.[19] We can see this reality in the physical structure of the tabernacle, where God met with the high priest in the cloud of incense over the mercy seat on the ark.[20] Praise elevates us to the place of God's presence where we can meet with him. The book of Hebrews shows us that as a result of Jesus' perfect sacrifice, when we pray we actually come before God's throne in heaven.[21] If this is true, it raises the question, "Where do we pray?" My body may be at the kitchen table at home, but because of the sacrifice of Christ and the presence of the Spirit within in me, my praying is actually before God's throne in heaven.

When God met Moses and Aaron from above the mercy seat over the ark, they came to know God more intimately.[22] God's presence in the tent also impacted Joshua. Exodus 33:11 says that God would "speak to Moses face to face, as a man speaks with his friend. Then Moses would return to the camp, but his young aide Joshua son of Nun did not leave the tent." This experience of God affected Joshua's "vision." Later, in Numbers 13 Joshua saw the same "giants" in the Promised Land that the other ten spies saw, yet he stood with Caleb and said, "The land we passed through and explored is exceedingly good. If the LORD is pleased with us, he will lead us into that land. . . . We should go up and take possession of the land, for we can certainly do it."[23]

Joshua's knowledge of God affected how he saw the threats in the Promised Land. Our knowledge of God affects how we see life. When we follow the example of Joshua and regularly enter the sanctuary where God is present, we too will see life from a different perspective. When the "giants" in our lives come into focus in the light of God's power and glory, we see them as they really are — grasshoppers. Worshipping God shapes our knowledge of him and sharpens our vision.

The bronze altar also informs the journey of knowing God. In chapter 5 we spoke of the altar as the place where we deal with self-will. A God who is holy will be known only on his terms, not on ours. The bronze altar is necessary in the quest of knowing God because at this altar we place ourselves in a posture of obedience to God. Obedience is a key to knowing God because it is an entryway into the experience of God. I can only know God to the extent that I am submitted to him, because it's only then that I will fully experience him. When I obey God I get into step with him and walk with him in life. Walking with God puts me in a position of closeness to him that allows me to know him.

In fact, Jesus says God will not disclose himself to just anyone, but to those who keep his Word.[24] The apostle John puts it more bluntly: "The man who says, 'I know him,' but does not do what he commands is a liar, and the truth is not in him."[25] When we obey God we express trust in him and step into a closer relationship with God where he will disclose himself to us more fully.

THE WAYS OF GOD

One of the most important quests in a life of devotion to God is coming to know his ways. God gives us a commentary on Israel's desert experience in Psalm 95:10: "For forty years I was angry with that generation; I said, 'They are a people whose hearts go astray, and they have not known my ways.'" God's conclusion was that his people's wandering loyalty was because they did not know his ways. David expands this theme in Psalm 103:7 where he compares Moses' knowledge of God with Israel's: "He made known his ways to Moses, his deeds to the people of Israel." Often in Hebrew poetry the writer uses two parts of a verse to play off of one another to make the message clear.

God's people knew him only in the acts of power God had demonstrated. They saw God kill the firstborn of the Egyptians and free them from 430 years of bondage, but when they were at the Red Sea being pursued by the Egyptian army, they assumed God had forsaken them.[26] When he parted the waters of the Red Sea, they were astonished; but a couple of months later in the desert when they were hungry, they accused God of starving them to death.[27] Later they were thirsty, and forgetting how God had cared for them, they accused him of causing them to die of thirst.[28] They saw the deeds of God but were not able to go beyond God's deeds to know his ways. When Israel was faced with a new challenge, they seemed unable to go beyond what they had seen God do. Their knowledge of God did not extend beyond the acts they observed.

Moses, on the other hand, went beyond the deeds of God to know his ways. So when Israel was pinned against the Red Sea, Moses didn't accuse God of abandoning his people, but said, "Do not be afraid. Stand firm and you will see the deliverance the LORD will bring you today."[29] Moses knew more than just what God had done in the past. He understood that God's ways are the patterns of his work in the world that reveal his character and his purposes. Those who press beyond God's deeds to know his ways find that in times of testing what they know about his character and purposes helps them to trust him with new uncertainties and challenges they face. They don't know how God will come through, but they know that his character and purposes can be trusted. Knowing the ways of God enables us to look at difficult situations with hope and anticipation of what God will do, instead of dreading disaster.

While God's ways are higher than our ways[30] and we can never fully know them,[31] he invites us into the inner sanctuary where we don't watch the pillar of cloud over the tabernacle but enter the Holiest of All, where God is waiting to disclose his ways to us. The psalmist shows us the path to knowing the ways of God. He cries out to God in frustration because of the prosperity of the wicked: "When I thought to know this, it was too painful for me; until I went into the sanctuary of God; then understood I their end."[32] For the psalmist, entering God's presence in the sanctuary meant coming into a place where God gave understanding of some of the perplexing ways in which he deals with people and their life circumstances. We can't attain this level of understanding of God from a distance. We have to be close enough to God to see it.

This is where worship helps us. When we worship God our praise brings us into closeness with God where we can observe and experience qualities of God that cannot be known at a distance. Worship, and praise in particular, helps us to know God because in worship we declare God's worth and focus our attention and affection on him.

But our worship must be authentic. Remember that the fire on the golden altar, the fire that ignites the incense into an ascending aroma, comes from the bronze altar. It is the fire of sacrifice in a life truly submitted to God that ignites our prayers, sending them before God's throne as a sweet aroma of incense to him. When we don't put to death self-will in our lives, it is like throwing water on the fire of our worship. God's throne is open to us, but before we can come to the golden altar we must first do business at the bronze altar.

When we offer God the sweet incense of our prayers and praise, he is present and gives us new insights into his purposes. But the ways of God are not formulas. They are not guarantees that if we do this, then God will do that. His ways are not tame. They describe God; they don't define him. There will always be a sense of mystery with God's ways; they are beyond us, but they are knowable.

RELATIONAL ATTRIBUTES

God is personal. This is why we can have a relationship with God. As God extends himself to us in relationship he makes it possible to have certain experiences of him. These experiences reveal qualities about our relationship with God, and how he relates to us. We could call them relational attributes, because they express ways in which we can know God in relationship. These attributes are pictures from our human world that help us understand how God wants us to experience him, how he relates to us.

We find them most easily in the psalms where these pictures of God are used with the personal pronouns "my" or "our" to describe God metaphorically. For instance, fifteen times in Psalms the writer says God offers us the opportunity to experience him as a refuge.[33] For instance Psalm 46:1,7,11 says, "God is our refuge" (KJV). The psalmists are inviting us to know and experience God as a refuge in life. We see many examples of relational attributes in Psalms: the Lord is my light and my salvation (27:1); my shepherd (23:1); my strength, my rock, my fortress, my deliverer, my God, my trust, my buckler, the horn of my salvation, and my strong tower (18:1-2). God is a refuge for us, a place we can enter and be safe. The tabernacle shows us how to enter the sanctuary of God's presence where we are safe from our enemies.[34]

Closing the door behind me quietly on a bright Tuskegee spring day, I knelt down on the worn carpet of my trailer and called out to the only One who could hear my prayer and help. I had just returned from a hard visit with the president of the university. He graciously agreed to meet me and a friend to discuss whether or not we would be admitted onto campus as a student organization. The meeting did not go well. I had left my home in Texas, moved to the Deep South, let go of my desire to pursue medicine, and now I couldn't even get on campus. On my knees and broken with nowhere to go, I called out to the One I knew would hear me from the sanctuary, "May the LORD answer you when you are in distress; may the name of the God of Jacob protect you. May he send you help from the sanctuary."[35]

So there, in my humble trailer, a mile outside of Tuskegee, Alabama, I entered the sanctuary of God's presence through gates of thanksgiving. I bowed before God and thanked him for the difficulty before me. This movement through the tabernacle in my mind would provide me with an opportunity to see God's power, because I knew there was nothing I could do. I went before the bronze altar to sacrifice afresh to God my commitment to stay right where I was, and not look for a way out, but look for God's way into the campus. I passed by the bronze laver to allow God's grace and love for me to wash away my growing sense of shame. I recalled that I didn't go to medical school; I disappointed my parents and had nothing to show them for the years of love and support they had poured into my life—nothing, that is, except an old trailer on a red clay lot. Only the grace of God could cleanse that gaping wound in my soul and make me a son they could be proud of.

Then, as I continued to feel the healing balm of God's love, I entered the Holy Place where I began to eat the Bread of Life from the golden table, as I meditated on Jesus, the Way. He is my Way to relationship with God; he is my Way to wholeness in life, and he is my Way onto campus in Tuskegee! I began to feel my strength return as I meditated on Scripture and fed my spirit and soul.[36] At the golden lampstand, I began to see the light in Jesus that would show me the way out of my despair. My confidence began to recharge as the light of God's Word inspired me, "Trust in the Lord with all your heart and lean not on your own understanding. In all your ways acknowledge him and he will direct your paths."[37] I could then turn to the golden altar and begin to praise God offering the incense of my prayer to him.

And as I praised and thanked God for meeting me in the sanctuary of my Tuskegee trailer, he met me and revealed something to me that I did not know. He spoke to me through his Word, there in the cloud of incense, my praise to him over the mercy seat of the ark of the covenant:[38] "Eddie, the name of the LORD is a strong tower; the righteous run to it and are safe."[39] Amazing! I understood that when I enter the name of the Lord as my strong tower, I am safe. In the midst of impossible situations, the name of God is my place of safety; and in the sanctuary of his presence, I am in the place where his name dwells.[40] The tabernacle was a spatial model that guided me into the presence of God, and in my pit of despair I came to know something about God that changed my life.

Knowing God is not just reading a passage of Scripture before work in the morning or doing a Sunday school lesson. It is meeting God in the heat of life and allowing him to show us things about himself he wants us to experience in moments of quiet and in hours of testing. The relational attributes of God are not just metaphors. They are ways we are to experience God in everyday life.

Worship is an integral part of knowing God, and our knowledge of God grows as we experience him by enjoying and submitting to his Word and his Spirit in the context of everyday life. So the tabernacle helps us approach God closely enough to behold his beauty, his character, his ways, and the ways he relates to us. Because worship and knowing God are everyday experiences, we turn next to look at how we find help in the sanctuary for everyday life.

CHAPTER 8

ONE THING HAVE I DESIRED
of the LORD

THE YEAR WAS 1976. I was a sophomore at Texas A&M University and attending a collegiate conference sponsored by The Navigators[1] just outside of the small west Texas town of Brownwood. The conference speaker was a seasoned Hispanic leader who accented his talks with a little Spanish, which fascinated me. After one of the sessions I visited with him and asked him to sign a copy of a small book that he had written.[2] When I looked at the booklet later, he had written a few words of encouragement to me and signed his name, but below that he had written the words, "Ps. 27:4." Friends had shared their special verses of Scripture with me before, but this was coming from an author and conference speaker!

That evening I took my Bible and looked up Psalm 27:4. It says, "One thing I ask of the LORD, this is what I seek: that I may dwell in the house of the LORD all the days of my life, to gaze upon the beauty of the LORD and to seek him in his temple." Something about that verse gripped me. Here was a king of Israel, a hero and champion, and the dynamo that energized his entire life was the habit of "dwelling in the house of the Lord." I began to wonder, "What's in there?" Why was that place so special for a king? A year later I discovered that the key to understanding why David wanted to dwell in the Lord's house was in the tabernacle.

DAVID AND THE TABERNACLE

Psalm 27:4 opens a window for us into the heart of this great king whose passion for God was legendary.[3] He says that the place he wanted to be was in the house of the Lord, and that this was the one thing he would do. Now, in David's day the temple was not yet built, so David would have pictured the "temple" in his mind in terms of the tabernacle of Moses. David's life was steeped in the imagery and mystique of the tabernacle.[4] The image of "dwelling in the house of the Lord" in David's heart would likely have been the interior of the tabernacle. Though David could not enter the Holy Place because he was not a priest, the imagery of the tabernacle filled David's heart and imagination.[5]

When he came before God in prayer, in his heart he was entering the Holy Place of the tabernacle. It was a spatial model of devotion for David. He knew that as the priest stepped beyond the blue, scarlet, and purple curtain he was in a different place. The familiar sights, sounds, and smells of the everyday world were gone, replaced by the exquisite serenity of the Holy Place. The priests left the world behind when they entered the tabernacle. David pursued this as a lifestyle. He made a habit of spending time alone with God, away from the pressures, responsibilities, and concerns of life. In the house of the Lord, he set aside the attentions of life for a while to be alone with God.

For David, the image of the inner sanctuary meant being in God's presence. When David emerged from the presence of God, he was different; he saw things differently. This was because David's perspective had changed. Perspective has to do with the position from which we are looking at an object. When we enter the sanctuary and God's presence, the experience of God changes the perspective from which we view life. My wife, Barbie, and I live in Colorado, and we enjoy hiking in the mountains. When we hike to the summit of 14,000-foot Pikes Peak, we notice how our perspective changes. The higher we hike up the mountain the more clearly we see the whole picture of our city. We can see our area of town and where it is in relation to other familiar places.

Our perspective changes as our altitude increases with each step toward the summit. From the top of the mountain we can see the whole world of our daily lives. We are often surprised by how different things look from altitude. The change in altitude allows us to see things in their correct proportion to each other. Some things that look big in everyday life appear small and insignificant from that height.

This is what entering into the house of the Lord did for David, and that's what our devotional life can do for us. Experiencing God's presence changes the altitude from which we live life. We can be so caught up in the pressures of everyday life that they distort our picture of reality. We live as though we are surrounded by massive nine-foot giants that we could never defeat. God invites us to follow the example of the psalmist of Israel and enter the inner sanctuary of God. There we can bask in his presence and enjoy him. When we emerge from that experience, we step back into life at a different altitude. We will see life differently.

Though David was young when he encountered Goliath, he had already begun to experience God in this intimate way.[6] He saw the massive nine-foot giant from a different perspective. David was young, and he had experienced God's presence in worship to the extent that it affected his vision. David was not looking at the giant from the perspective of a teenage boy on earth, but from the vantage point of God Most High in heaven who looked down on this enemy of Israel as a speck of dust. David's perspective was a result of the secret place he had already found. And what was that secret place like?

THE BEAUTY OF GOD

The next phrase of Psalm 27:4 satisfies this curiosity. David describes two things he does in the sanctuary. The first is to behold the beauty of the Lord. "To behold" here means to look at something with intensity and gratification.[7] When David entered the sanctuary, his focus was on the Lord, and he found deep satisfaction in the Lord himself. There is a need in our lives to have times when we focus on the Lord himself. These are times when we are not preoccupied with other things, but are free to focus our attention only on the Lord. David developed this habit in life, and the Scripture invites us to nurture the regular habit of spending focused time alone with God, looking intently at him. When David recalls his time in the sanctuary, it's the beauty of God that he remembers. Even though the beauty of God is not mentioned often in Scripture,[8] when it appears the scenery is rich.

The beauty of God is a way of describing his perfection. When something is beautiful, it has a sense of completeness about it; it is pleasing; it is the perfect example of the way something should be. When we say a work of art is beautiful, we mean that a painter uses color, texture, value, and a host of other techniques to perfectly portray a subject. The result is alluring, captivating, and if it is truly beautiful, it is inspiring. God is the supreme example of perfection. To dwell even for a short time in the presence of perfection not only washes the dulling effects of our unsafe and imperfect world from us but also places before us an object that is truly worthy of adoration.

The natural response to beauty is worship. When we see a beautiful person or a breathtaking scene in nature, we are overcome with awe and admiration. We want to declare its worth. So when we enter the Holiest of All to behold the beauty of the Lord, we come before the One whose beauty is the perfect figure of which all other forms of beauty are imperfect reflections. The beauty of God is inspiring because in God we see reality as it should be. The perfection of God calls out to what is distorted or missing in our souls and creates a longing for what can be. It draws us to the One who can complete us and make whole the imperfect and broken areas in our souls.

Though we cannot have perfection now, when we enter life in Jesus Christ we get the first satisfying glimpses of the beauty of God, foretastes of the fullness we will enjoy one day with God. Abstract artist Makoto Fujimura says that beauty rehumanizes humanity.[9] The entrance of sin into the world leached from our souls and our world much of the beauty and glory there. It robbed us of much of what it meant to be fully human. Beholding God's perfection bathes our soul in his beauty and washes us with the hope of one day being like him. Though we do not enter this perfection now, in Christ we begin to taste and see the beauty that we will experience in its fullness one day. Perfection creates desire in the heart of the beholder. God is so pleasing in all of his qualities that to get a glimpse of him kindles a passion for him in our hearts.

In Scripture, we see two qualities of God tied to his beauty. The Old Testament directly connects God's beauty and his holiness four times.[10] We are told to worship the Lord in the beauty of his holiness. God's holiness is described as beautiful. This means that in all that he is God is separate from all imperfection and sin. His holiness is so perfect that it is the highest, purest pleasure human desire can experience. The image Scripture gives for understanding the experience of God's presence in worship is the Holiest of All. God's presence is in a place that is called the Most Holy Place because the One who inhabits it is the supreme example of perfection and is absolutely without comparison in heaven or on earth. We are invited to worship God in a place we could never gain access to on our own, the throne room of the eternal God whose presence is the perfection of beauty and holiness.

Beauty and glory also appear together describing God.[11] The main idea underlying the word *glory* in Hebrews is the sense of weight or heaviness.[12] God's glory is not only the weighty sense of awe associated with all that he is, including qualities like his power, love, truth, immensity, and knowledge, but it is the overwhelming brilliance of his beauty. Glory and beauty belong together in describing God because glory speaks of the intensity of his beauty and beauty shows the splendor of his glory. At the dedication of both the tabernacle and the temple of Solomon, God's presence filled the sanctuary with such brilliant glory that the priests could not enter. The shimmering beauty of these sanctuaries was filled with the glory of God so that no one could even enter them.[13]

SEEKING GOD

God's beauty ignited David's passion for him and inspired his perseverance during the difficult years of his life. But the beauty of God was not all that David needed in the sanctuary. He mentions something else important to him in the sanctuary—inquiring of God. During David's life he made a habit of seeking God for wisdom and direction when he needed it. Time and time again David went to God for wisdom in battle, and when he inquired of the Lord, God answered him.[14] The sanctuary was the place he knew he could find wisdom for the life-threatening decisions before him.

It is not surprising for a person like David, who loved God, to be drawn to the tabernacle as a place to seek God. Even from the days of the judges when Israel needed wisdom from God, they went to the sanctuary to find it. The house of God was where the ark of the covenant rested, and there dwelt God's representative throne on earth[15] where they could come before him to understand his will. Though we don't need a tabernacle to seek God today, this living parable of approaching God still gives us a picture of how to meet God when we need his direction.

There was a secret to David's success as king. At the very center of his life was a burning passion to know God and to be led by him. David wanted to please God, and he knew that he couldn't do that in his own power. He needed the inspiration and renewal that came from reveling in the beauty of the Lord to handle the pressures of kingship. The presence of God altered David's perspective of life, enabling him to see problems more from the vantage point of heaven than earth. When faced with perplexing or dire circumstances, David knew that there was a place he could go to find the wisdom he needed for everything from military strategy to dealing with a famine.[16]

David's example can be as useful to a working mother with small children at home as it is to the plumber struggling to see his business survive. From the hourly employee to the corporate executive, we all need the restorative radiance of God's beauty to replenish what the pressures of everyday life leach from us. Seeking God himself is the path of abundant life. We can come into the sanctuary of his presence to inquire of God and find direction for the weighty and often perplexing decisions we face. Seeking God's desire for our lives is such an important subject, let's look at it in more detail.

CHAPTER 9

THE JOURNEY of DISCERNING GOD'S WILL

I STARED AT the massive eight-foot-tall stone fireplace feeling as if my comfortable little nest was being dismantled. I was standing in the Great Hall, a stately meeting room in the nineteenth-century Tudor-style castle that serves as the centerpiece of The Navigators' international home in Colorado. I had recently graduated from seminary and was unsure of what was next. One thing was sure—whatever I did next would not be in Russia!

I had just finished listening to a stunning account of what God was doing in the former Soviet Union. Dr. Bruce Wilkinson, then president of Walk Thru the Bible, had shared one riveting story after another of the work of God's Spirit in the lives of people and institutions in what was then called the Commonwealth of Independent States. An unprecedented door of opportunity was opening for the gospel of Jesus Christ in the former Soviet Union, and a growing partnership across the body of Christ in the United States was rapidly forming to respond to it. So there I stood, surrounded by the bustling excitement of a movement being born, and I was being swept up in it.

The next morning as I boarded a flight for Chicago to return to my life there, I felt deeply unsettled. The experience in the Great Hall had jarred me, and I felt that God was nudging me in a new direction, but

I wasn't sure I wanted to hear what he had to say. I had invested the last four years of my life in completing graduate studies in the New Testament and learning to speak Spanish as a member of a wonderful community of believers from El Salvador, Panama, Paraguay, Peru, and Mexico. I was quite content there. The last thing I wanted to consider was that God might be uprooting me and transplanting me in Russia. As this tension grew within me, I began to wrestle with the question, how would I know if God is leading me to Russia? There are times in life when we need God's wisdom to know what to do, what choice to make, whether or not we should take a bold step and leave behind what's familiar for a new world. God has provided a path of wisdom to guide us in times like these.

It is especially in the deserts of our lives that we need direction from God. After I moved to Russia and found myself in another desert experience, I would take long walks in Moscow's Bitsevsky Park. On those strolls I would cry out, "Lord, if you would just show me what to do, I would do it." But there was nothing but silence. God's ways are higher than ours. In desperate times, I just want to know what to do. I want to know what can be done to fix my situation and relieve the pain. But I've realized that God wants to transform me through the process, not just give me an answer I may not be ready to receive. God doesn't just drop answers into our lap, he transforms us so that we can handle the new pressures they bring. This, too, is one of God's ways. The tabernacle helps us in the journey of knowing God's will.

A PATH FOR SEEKING GOD'S WILL

We enter his gates with thanksgiving. The path of seeking God's will begins with God, not a need or an issue. Psalm 100:4 says to enter his gates with thanksgiving and his courts with praise. We are to give thanks in all situations, even the desert.[1] This is important, because in order to praise and thank God, I must know and trust in something about God that is bigger than my situation. Psalm 100:5 goes on to say, "The LORD is good and his love endures forever; his faithfulness continues through all generations." This is why we can enter the gates that lead to the Lord's presence with thanksgiving, because no matter what we face we can know that the Lord is good, that his love has no limit, and that he is faithful. This does not give us the answers we want when we are hurting, but it does point us to the character of God, who can be trusted even when life doesn't make sense and we are hurting and the pain won't go away.

One thing that certainly blocks my ability to understand God's desire for me is self-will. This is why our first stop on the path of seeking God's will is at the bronze altar. When we put to death self-will, we follow the example of Jesus in the garden the night before he faced a horrible death. He prayed, "Father, if you are willing, take this cup from me; yet not my will, but yours be done" (Luke 22:42). Before his betrayer arrived, Jesus settled the issue of whose will was in charge. He yielded his will to the Father.[2] Jesus showed us how to deal with self-will. First, he poured his heart out to the Father and asked if there was any way out of the horrific pain ahead. Here Jesus demonstrated that it is a healthy thing to pour out our hearts to God, including our pain and struggles.[3] But notice that Jesus went on to say, "Not my will but yours be done." In the face of unspeakable pain he laid aside his will and accepted the will of the Father, even when it meant a very painful road. The first step in understanding the will of God is being committed to following it. A broken and contrite heart is what God desires in us,[4] and with this heart we can approach him.

While the bronze altar guides us to deal with self-will, the laver points to the cleansing of my inner world so that I can see clearly; the pure in heart will see God.[5] Here God invites me to be cleansed of the motives and attitudes that will block me from being able to see the Lord's will. These include at least five sins that must be cleansed from our inner life. The first is unforgiveness. When we don't forgive others, we delay our own healing and block the flow of God's grace and blessing into our lives.[6] A second sin is bitterness, which poisons our inner life and our relationships with others.[7] When I am bitter against another person, I have not forgiven him or her but have usually been stewing over an offense. I must come to the place of forgiving the person to move closer to God.

Another sin is anger, which does not please God but indicates that something is not right within us. If the anger is not dealt with, it can give the Devil a foothold in our lives.[8] A fourth sin to cleanse our inner person of is jealousy. When we are so fixed on the desirable qualities or accomplishments of others, we can find ourselves angry at another person because of his or her successes and blessings. Jealousy can also cause bitterness. With jealousy brewing in our heart, it's difficult to see clearly what God wants us to do. It is a short step from jealousy to the fifth sin, covetousness. Paul calls covetousness idolatry.[9] Coveting something or someone means that our desire for that person or thing is extreme, unreasonable, and has no concern for the needs of another. I cannot pursue what God wants when my soul is grasping tightly to something that I've decided I want. These are five examples of sins that can spoil the process of seeking God if we don't cleanse our hearts of them.

When we've finished the work of cleansing, we are ready to enter the Lord's presence with a better posture of brokenness and holiness. The golden lampstand calls our attention to the source of light in decision making. In chapter 6 we saw that the lampstand was the only source of light in the tabernacle. God is our light, and he sent Jesus into the world to be the true light. Jesus guides us by his light through the Word of God.[10] In facing a decision, Scripture will not tell us which job to take or which person to marry, but God's Word does shine light on aspects of the decision that help us. For example, Scripture provides us at least three kinds of light that can guide us in decision making: principles of wisdom, qualities of God, and promises of God.

Principles of wisdom point us to the way of wisdom and can keep us out of trouble in decisions we face. In a decision several years ago, I realized that the wisest choice was also the most difficult one. I did not feel I was ready to face that degree of risk. While praying one day, Hebrews 10:38 came to mind: "But my righteous one will live by faith. And if he shrinks back, I will not be pleased with him." This verse of Scripture shined God's light on the fear in my heart and challenged me to trust God, not shrink back, and do what was difficult because a life of faith pleases God.

Qualities of God include his attributes and the ways he works in our lives. In August of 1996 I faced a weighty decision: Do I ask Barbie to marry me? The more I thought about the responsibilities of marriage, the more questions I had. Would she be able to leave her friends, family, and familiar world of nursing to join me in full-time ministry in a different part of the country? Where would she be vulnerable, and though we had discussed it, how would she handle the unique pressures of my world of ministry? After days of tossing this over and over in my mind, I shared my dilemma with a wise friend and mentor, and he made a comment that changed everything. He said, "Well, Eddie, Ecclesiastes 3:14 says, 'I know that everything God does will endure forever; nothing can be added to it and nothing taken from it. God does it so that men will revere him.'"

That verse stunned me, and I stopped in the midst of my wrestling. When God does something it will endure. As I reflected on this verse, I began to see that being responsible does not mean eliminating risk, it means trusting God with the hard questions of life. I understood that if God is leading in our relationship, nothing needs to be added to Barbie or me, or taken away from us. God would use each of our strengths and weaknesses to test us and mature our relationship for his glory, that people would see it and revere God. Three months later Barbie and I were married on November 23, 1996, and we are still discovering ways we complement each other for God's glory.

The promises of God[11] are a third kind of light God's Word provides to guide us. God's promises are statements about his character and his purposes that he invites us to hold to and believe in, especially in times of change, suffering, and uncertainty. God's promises can also express qualities of our relationship with God that he desires us to experience and to trust. For example, "The LORD is my shepherd; I shall not want" (Psalm 23:1, KJV); or "The LORD is my light and my salvation; whom shall I fear?" (Psalm 27:1, KJV). These are relational attributes of God that we are to trust and experience. In seeking God's will, what we often need is the confidence to do what our heart tells us God is saying to us as we pray. Often this confidence comes to us in the form of a promise of God we can depend on as we face a decision.

A year after Barbie and I were married, The Navigators asked us to consider serving on the National Leadership Team of The U.S. Navigators. I had no national leadership experience at that time, but after praying much about this opportunity, we felt it was right. Although my heart told me yes, I didn't have the confidence to make the decision. In prayer one day, Isaiah 41:10 came to mind: "So do not fear, for I am with you; do not be dismayed, for I am your God. I will strengthen you and help you; I will uphold you with my righteous right hand." When I read this verse in the midst of the pressure of this decision, I felt the power of this truth more deeply and clearly than ever. God promised that he would be with me, he would be my God, he would help me, and he would uphold me with his power. The promises of God can activate our faith and help us respond to him in a manner that pleases him.[12] We accepted the role, moved to The Navigators' headquarters in Colorado, and began a journey that has taken us to deeper experiences of God.

While Christ sends his light to us through his Word, he also provides light for us through the horizontal dimension of people. Scripture speaks about the importance of advice from spiritually mature, godly, and wise men and women who can give us objective feedback when we are facing a decision.[13] Counsel works best when a trusted person points out something we've overlooked, something we're not seeing clearly, or something new we haven't considered. Counsel provides us practical wisdom for the process of decision making, as my mentor did for me when he shared Ecclesiastes 3:14.

The golden altar of incense speaks to the importance of prayer in decision making. God encourages us to come to him when we lack wisdom and to ask for it.[14] In the perplexing pressures of a decision, we can easily forget that it is God who knows the end from the beginning,[15] and he wants us to come to him to know his will. As we come to God in prayer to seek his will, it's important to remember there are two sides of prayer: asking and listening. Our prayer is not to be a one-sided phone conversation, where one person does all the talking but doesn't listen. In prayer before the throne of God, we not only come and make our requests known but also watch and listen for what God has to say. And he speaks — through his Word, through others, and through a variety of creative means to give us the direction we need.

The ark of the covenant with its mercy seat represents the very throne of God we approach in prayer.[16] Using this sacred furnishing as a model for seeking God's will, we can discover several important principles. The ark of the covenant was the point of intersection between heaven and earth; it was the place where these two worlds met. In the decision-making process, the ark represents the place I come to make my decision, the throne of God. When Moses or Aaron went into God's presence within the tabernacle, the tent of meeting, or on the mountain,[17] they went in alone. While I receive counsel from others as an important part of a decision, when I actually make the decision I stand before God alone, because it is to God I will give account for my life, which includes the life-shaping decisions I make.[18] Coming before God is an expression of my dependence on him, not on my abilities to reason or figure things out. As such, I depend on the Holy Spirit to guide my process of decision. The Spirit of God is referred to as the Spirit of wisdom and revelation.[19] The Holy Spirit guides us into God's wisdom as we depend on him. He also reveals to us what we need to know about how we can please God and link our story to the grand story of his will.

The Spirit of God operates in another way when we try to discern God's will. When we seek God's will, one fruit of the Spirit is particularly important: the fruit of peace.[20] Often times I have seen in my life and the lives of others who are making decisions that we just don't seem to have peace in our hearts about a choice that might otherwise seem right. The Holy Spirit gives the fruit of peace, or withholds it. When we face a decision and lack peace in our hearts, it's wise to pay attention to this and to ask God: "Why?"

Just before I went to Tuskegee, I had an opportunity to pursue graduate study at one of the leading seminaries in the country. Everything lined up—everything, that is, except peace. In my heart, something was just not right about this choice. I brought my lack of peace to God in prayer, and a week or so later I was speaking with an elder mentor who pointed me to Ecclesiastes 8:5: "Whoever obeys his command will come to no harm, and the wise heart will know the right time and procedure." When I looked at this verse, I realized there is a right time and a right procedure for everything. As I prayed over that reality, I began to feel God's peace flood into my heart. Graduate studies might be the right procedure, but this was not the right time. That proved to be a wise decision for me, and ten years later I did complete a three-year graduate degree from another excellent school.

Finally, the act of making the decision is an act of faith. Hebrews 11:6 says that without faith it is impossible to please God. Decision making is a great place to express our faith and give pleasure to God. In most cases, decisions involve risk. This means I don't know how the situation will work out before I decide. When I come to the point of making the decision I take a step of faith, and the best place to take that step is in the presence of God, at his throne. In my human frailty and limited vision I say to God, "Lord, as best I can tell this choice is pleasing to you, and by faith I choose it now before you. I am imperfect, so I commit this choice to you and trust you that if it is best you will affirm it, and if not you will redirect me." And then I walk by faith and in humility, looking for God's continual leading. Even the apostle Paul tried twice to take the gospel to different places, and each time the Holy Spirit prevented him.[21] I don't have to get it right the first time. I can trust the Spirit of God to lead me, just as he led Paul, to the best choice to please God.

The tabernacle can serve as a model for seeking God when we need him most. It was this model that guided me in making two of the biggest decisions of my life: to go to Russia and to marry Barbie.

David says that in the house of the Lord he wants to behold the beauty of the Lord and to inquire of him. The sanctuary was where David went to inquire of God. The tabernacle can serve as a model for making some of life's most important decisions. But life can still be difficult at times. We can find ourselves in desert seasons where we despair even of life. In times like these one thing we need is hope. But how do we find hope in the desert? Let's find out.

CHAPTER 10

AN ANCHOR for OUR SOUL

IN THE DESERT seasons of life, at some point our circumstances begin to wear us down. They are like the thunderstorms that used to pound us day after day in the late summers of my childhood on the Texas Gulf Coast. Bad news, a crushing word, failure, watching someone else get chosen to do something I had hoped to do, or seeing someone else receive the award and praise I longed to experience. Or maybe it's just being overlooked . . . again. When these experiences come in waves, they can hit us with a disorienting force that begins to twist our view of reality.

When I'm worn down by waves of discouragement, I become vulnerable to the voices of the Enemy and my flesh. These voices accuse me of weakness, magnify my faults and failures, and eventually begin to sound like my own. They take the wounded areas of my heart, those not yet healed by Jesus, and use them as a lens to distort reality. They paint a picture of my life that tells me I can never win, and I might not even survive. This is the point where we begin to lose hope. We can live without a lot of things, but we can't live long without hope. There is a way of hope in the desert, a path that leads out of the labyrinth of despair to an anchor in the storm.

A PICTURE OF HOPE

The idea of hope in the Old Testament is carried primarily by four words in Hebrew: קָוָה (kaw·vaw), יָחַל (yaw·chal), חָכָה (khaw·kaw), and שָׂבַר (saw·bar).[1] Together they paint a picture of anticipation and expectation. Hope is an attitude of expectation that creates a posture of waiting. There is such a close relationship between the ideas of waiting and hoping in Hebrew that the same verb is translated "wait" in some English versions and "hope" in others.[2] To hope means to anticipate something with such confidence that a person is willing to wait patiently for it. The confidence of hope comes from the sure knowledge upon which it is based.[3]

In the New Testament we find a similar idea expressed in the word ἐλπίς (el·pece), which means to anticipate something with a good reason for confident expectation.[4] Hope is not a whimsical wish that has no rooting in reality. Hope, in fact, is like an anchor.

THE ANCHOR BEYOND THE VEIL

Again we turn to the book of Hebrews to take us deep into the substance of the hope we have in Jesus Christ. Hebrews was written to a small community of suffering believers.[5] Hebrews shows us that hope is not wishful thinking but reality that I can hold on to. And it's hope that anchors me in ultimate reality when life hits me with waves of disappointment and discouragement. Hope in Hebrews is not the act of hoping; it is the objective reality for which one hopes.[6] In Hebrews 3:6, hope is the root of our confidence under pressure, enabling us to hold on to courage and remain faithful to what we say we believe. Hope gives us a certainty that distinguishes us from others who are suffering without it (Hebrews 6:11). In chapter 7, hope is described as the objective reality of the new and living way Jesus opened into the presence of God (verse 19). And the author tells us in Hebrews 10:23 to hold on to the confession of our hope because God's promise is trustworthy, and he is faithful. In each case, hope is pointing to a reality that holds us firm during times of testing and uncertainty.

The most vivid picture of hope in the book of Hebrews is in chapter 6: "We have this hope as an anchor for the soul, firm and secure. It enters the inner sanctuary behind the curtain."[7] In this unusual image, we are told that hope is an anchor for our soul. This imagery is not uncommon around the Mediterranean Sea where literature uses the metaphor of an anchor to describe something that gives stability and security.[8] It was the weight of God's character that made his promises secure (Hebrews 6:13-18). Because God could find no one greater, he swore by himself to fulfill his word to Abraham and his descendants. This hope is certain because it is rooted in the unchangeable character and purposes of God and the work of his Son Jesus as the High Priest of the new covenant.[9] So this hope anchors the soul of God's people, but again we find another twist in the story. In the middle of this gripping nautical image, the author of Hebrews switches metaphors and goes to the tabernacle for imagery to describe how the anchor of hope works.

In order for an anchor to work it must be hooked on something that doesn't move. When a boat stops, the captain lowers the anchor to hook it on something immovable. If the captain lowers the anchor ten feet and stops it, leaving the anchor hanging in forty feet of water, the anchor is suspended in the same medium the boat is floating in — the ocean. In this case, the boat is not secure because the anchor is not attached to something that can hold the boat. This picture describes why so many in our current generation are adrift without hope. It's because their lives are "anchored" in the same medium we are floating in — the world around us. Our lives cannot be secure if they are anchored in the same ocean of human reality we are floating in everyday.

It's too easy to anchor our hope in our jobs, our appearance, our families, our money, our abilities, our knowledge, our skills, or our influence. These things are good, but they are not dependable and will never be able to hold us. The currents of life come along and sweep away a job, take away health, reduce our abilities, and show us that with all our knowledge or influence we can't make things turn out the way we'd like. The message is this—our hope must be anchored beyond the ocean of life where we are floating for us to be secure. For a boat to be secure the anchor must be hooked beyond the ocean to the bottom. For our hope to be secure it must be hooked beyond the world we live in.

This is exactly what the author of Hebrews tells us. He says, "We have this hope as an anchor for the soul, firm and secure. It enters the inner sanctuary behind the curtain, where Jesus, who went before us, has entered on our behalf."[10] The author returns to the image of the tabernacle, focusing on the veil between the Holy Place and the Holiest of All. He says that our hope is an anchor that goes beyond the veil and enters the Holiest of All, where Jesus entered before us. What is this saying? The author of Hebrews is picking up a theme he introduced in Hebrews 4:14 where he describes Jesus as "great high priest who has gone through the heavens." It is a subject he will develop more fully in chapters 8 and 9 where he shows that the tabernacle is a spatial model of heaven itself where Jesus will enter.[11]

The veil is a boundary. It marks the limit beyond which we cannot go. In the old covenant the outer veil at the door of the tabernacle marked a boundary; if you were not a priest you could not enter. The inner veil marked another boundary beyond which only the high priest could go, and then only once a year.[12] Here in Hebrews 6:19-20, the veil and the Holiest of All refer to the place Jesus went ahead of us, into heaven.[13] Our anchor of hope must be set beyond the limits of human experience in the realm of ultimate reality. The author of Hebrews gives us an expression of ultimate reality into which our anchor of hope must hook. We have already seen that Hebrews draws a spatial connection between heaven and earth. The tabernacle is on earth, but it points to ultimate reality in heaven, the heavenly sanctuary and God's throne.

We live on earth, but the tabernacle offers us a way of taking our hope beyond the veil of earthly limitations into heaven itself. When we anchor our hope in heaven, it means that in the struggles of our lives on earth we are not limited to the resources of earth. The resources available to us are not only what we can feel, smell, taste, touch, and see. When God answers from heaven, he answers out of the riches of heaven, which are not limited to what we can see from our finite vantage point on earth. Our hope is not anchored in our familiar earthly world, but far beyond it in the heavenly world that is unshakeable.[14]

HOPE AND HELP

To be credible, hope must offer us something we need. One thing we need in times of testing is help. Often in these times we don't even know what we need. It's then that we need to know that God is our help. This is a prominent theme in the book of Psalms. Look at these passages:

We wait in hope for the LORD; he is our help and our shield. (33:20)

God is our refuge and strength, an ever-present help in trouble. (46:1)

Because you are my help, I sing in the shadow of your wings. (63:7)

I will lift up mine eyes unto the hills, from whence cometh my help. (121:1, KJV)

My help cometh from the LORD, which made heaven and earth. (121:2, KJV)

Our help is in the name of the LORD, who made heaven and earth. (124:8, KJV)

The Lord is our help! But how do we get to the Lord to receive his help? How do we find him? David says, "May he send you help from the sanctuary and grant you support from Zion."[15] The sanctuary was the place where David found help from the Lord. The tabernacle shows us the path to God's presence, and in his presence we will find what we need. Psalm 96:6 tells us that "strength and beauty"[16] are in his sanctuary. In the place God's presence dwells we expect to experience the qualities of his character. The psalmist says that two attributes of God we experience in his presence are his strength and beauty. We discussed beauty in chapter 8, so now we turn to strength. When we find ourselves in a desert season of life, one thing we need is strength. Whether it's physical, emotional, psychological, intellectual, or spiritual strength, sometimes in the desert we just need to make it through the day or night. It's times like these that the tabernacle points us to the way of help.

Hebrews 4:16 unveils how we can find strength in the sanctuary: "Let us then approach the throne of grace with confidence, so that we may receive mercy and find grace to help us in our time of need." The author exhorts us to come boldly to God's throne of grace to find the mercy and grace we need. He uses the sanctuary to give us a way of thinking about where to go for help in difficult times. It is the grace and mercy of God that give us strength to persevere. When God offers us strength in the sanctuary, it's not feel-good pop psychology. He is giving us something of substance to help us! Grace is not only God's unmerited favor, it is the capacity we need to do what God desires of us.

We see this in Paul's use of this word *grace* in the book of Ephesians where he says that it was the grace of God that gave him the capacity to preach the unsearchable riches of Jesus.[17] The word for gift, *charisma*, is a form of the word grace, *charis*. A spiritual gift is a special capacity from God that enables us to do what God has perfectly designed us to contribute to his body and his mission in the world. When the apostle Paul suffered a unique torment in his life, the Lord said to him, "My grace is sufficient for you, for my power is made perfect in weakness." Then Paul concludes, "Therefore I will boast all the more gladly about my weaknesses, so that Christ's power may rest on me."[18] Jesus told Paul that in times of testing it is the grace of God that gives him strength to persevere.

We experience and express God's strength most powerfully in our weakness. We know that grace and humility are closely related in Scripture. God resists the proud and gives grace to the humble.[19] God is near to the brokenhearted and to those who have a contrite spirit.[20]

When we come to the throne of God, it is a throne of grace! He is the God of all grace[21] who is ready to bestow his grace on those whose hearts are humble and broken before him. And this is a frequent condition of our hearts in the desert where what we have been depending on is stripped from us.

Mercy is the kindness and concern that God has for those in need.[22] It is God's mercy that moves him to help us when we are in distress. If God was not merciful, he would just stand by, watch us in pain, and do nothing. His mercy moves him with compassion to help us when we are struggling.[23] In one of the lowest ebbs of Israel's history, the prophet Jeremiah writes to the people of God, "It is of the LORD's mercies that we are not consumed, because his compassions fail not. They are new every morning: great is thy faithfulness."[24] In the midst of periods of prolonged testing, every morning we awake to God's mercies and compassions waiting to greet us. God's mercy does not usually remove the pain when we want, but it brings the companionship of God to us in the midst of our hurt. In his mercy, God sustains us in ways we feel but don't fully understand.

In chapter 7 I described one spring day in Tuskegee when I was frustrated and at the end of my rope as I prayed. I had just left a discouraging meeting with the president of the university and had no idea what to do next. A few days later I was walking across campus and ran into one of the dorm directors. He invited me to help him create a program for the dorms he supervised. That program resulted in a Bible study in the freshman dorm where many students came to faith in Christ.

Coming to the sanctuary is finding a place of hope, because in the sanctuary we connect with the God of heaven and his resources. In the sanctuary a universe of possibilities we could never imagine opens to us—because God is there. I could never have imagined the solution God brought me in Tuskegee, because I don't know the limitless resources of God. And I don't have to know them—I just need to know the Lord of heaven and be able to find him. He possesses the resources and the wisdom for their best use. The sanctuary is a place of hope because it is there we find the God of hope. The God of grace and mercy is there waiting for us.

HOPE AND HOME

During my time in Russia, when everything around me was so different from life in America, my heart struggled to find something familiar. I thought often in those days of how much I missed my home. My childhood memories were forged in the heat of the civil rights movement of the 1960s in Houston, Texas. We grew up only a few blocks from Texas Southern University, a historically black university that experienced rioting during those years. In seventh and eighth grades I went to an inner-city junior high school. On Monday mornings at school we would hear the stories of "who the gangs got" over the weekend, and we would wonder who would be next. My brother Ken and one of our friends had to jump out of a window at the junior high school he attended when someone started shooting in the hallway. Life was often threatening and scary, but when my ten-year-old frame walked through the door of 3328 Parkwood Drive, I was home. Home was the place I could go that would "make everything all right." In many of the games we play as children, the object is to make it to home base; when you make it "home," you are safe!

But I was six thousand miles from home, and God was taking me to a new place of refuge. The tabernacle gave me a real model of my eternal home, the throne room of my heavenly Father. It is a place where I am always safe, in his presence. Right there in Red Square, in the snow and biting cold, it was as if the spatial reality of God's presence surrounded me. The model of the tabernacle gave me something familiar. There in his presence I could eat the bread of his Word and offer the incense of praise to him; I could be quiet and be quieted in the light of his countenance from the candlestick and ultimately come before the wings of the cherubim into the very throne room of God himself—to God, my exceeding joy[25]—and I could do that in humble contrition before God right on the gray stones of Red Square.

A SURE HOPE

Hope is an anchor for our souls because it connects our lives to the unchangeable, unshakable reality of heaven itself. Christ has gone before us to take his seat on the throne of heaven until the day all his enemies are destroyed and his reign fully comes.[26] Jesus anchored us in the reality of a new covenant relationship. He forged this relationship with the God of heaven for us by his perfect sacrifice. The marvelous salvation he obtained for us[27] gives us bold access to the very throne of God in heaven. The hope that anchors us in life is not dependent on the shifting currents of this present world but on the unchangeable nature of God and his promise,[28] which finds its perfect expression in the life and sacrifice of his Son, Jesus.

When we suffer in this world we endure hardship differently than others. Our hope helps us to suffer differently than others because our soul is anchored in a different place than the world around us. This hope produces a life with a contagious curiosity about it. People cannot explain the joy, strength, and peace of a person whose life has this hope as an anchor.[29] Hope gives us a future that changes the way we see the present, especially when we suffer. We have hope because Jesus connects us with God through a new relationship that opens to us the resources of heaven in our times of need.

Our hope is an anchor for the soul that is real. Far from being wishful thinking, our hope is anchored in the very nature of God himself and in the work of his Son, Jesus, on our behalf. Our hope, in fact, is in Jesus, the Son of God who is seated on the right hand of God now praying for us. We turn next to look at what Jesus has accomplished in the great salvation he offers us.

CHAPTER 11

A CROWN of BEAUTY

THE DESERT IS a place to see great beauty. The arid monotony of sand and cactus paints a background that makes beauty jump out at you, like a purple flower on a bland desert floor. I experienced this during my first year in Moscow. In the midst of the loneliness and failure of my own desert experience, I decided to visit the Bolshoi Theatre. I had been to the ballet back in the States, but I was eager to visit the legendary Bolshoi. I caught the metro down to the Teatralnaya station and got off for the frigid, seven-minute walk through the blowing snow to Russia's premier ballet theater.

After squeezing through the entrance with five hundred other guests, my senses were barraged with beauty everywhere. The plush ruby carpeting led me down a chandelier-studded hallway into the main auditorium. When I entered the theater, I had to stop to take in the three-story crystal chandelier surrounded by ornate, gold-trimmed balconies before taking my seat. The Bolshoi Theatre Symphony Orchestra struck up the opening line of *Lebedínoye Ózero* (*Swan Lake*) and I was mesmerized. The curtain lifted and the combined effect of the music, the dance, the scenery on stage, and the decor of the Bolshoi itself saturated my senses with a panorama of beauty I'd never experienced before. In the midst of the parched condition of my soul, I experienced the kind of exuberant burst of life that follows a desert rain.

At once I realized that the beauty of the Bolshoi was pointing me to the Beauty of God himself. I thought to myself: *Who is it that gave Russian architects the imagination to create the Bolshoi Theatre? Where did Pyotr Ilyich Tchaikovsky find the passion and insight to write* Swan Lake? *From where do Mikhail Barishnikov and other world-class Russian ballet artists get the grace and strength to bound across the stage with pirouettes and leaps that dazzle audiences from around the world?* It was to the author of Beauty that I turned as this wave of inspiration washed over me. I was surprised to find beauty in a most unsuspecting place, in the middle of my desert experience.

This is a parable for life. God displays his beauty most vividly when he does so against a backdrop of darkness and even pain. This is true nowhere more profoundly than with the subject of salvation. The magnitude of the goodness and beauty of salvation is clearest against the backdrop of the evil, pain, and sadness that make it necessary. Sin places the entire human race in a state of brokenness and disrepair that we cannot fix.[1] Furthermore, the presence of sin in our lives bears with it the dire price tag of death. Death is the consequence for sin, and because God is just, death is the only acceptable payment for sin.[2] As we mentioned in chapter 5, the entire sacrificial system of the tabernacle is an unpleasant picture of God's attitude toward sin and his solution for it. Innocent animals were sacrificed and their blood used to cover the sins of the nation of Israel for a year.[3]

It was only after the ugliness of blood and sacrifice that the priests could experience the beauty of God's presence. The book of Hebrews casts some interesting light on the subject of salvation and helps us to understand that our salvation is not just for later, it is for now.

SALVATION THROUGH THE EYES OF HEBREWS

For the author of Hebrews, the believer's salvation was not as much a past-tense event as a present and future reality.[4] The perfect offering of

Jesus not only gives us reason to wait expectantly for his return and our complete release from sin[5] but also gives us the possibility of a whole new life when we embrace him in faith.

In the book of Hebrews, salvation is portrayed largely through the language of covenant.[6] A covenant is a binding agreement that establishes a relationship between two parties and the terms of their relationship. The old covenant placed the people of God in a relationship with him that had to be mediated by priests. The people could not go directly to God: The priests had to represent them. Their sins were forgiven, but the resulting relationship was distant.

Salvation in the new covenant opened up a very different relationship with God. Jesus, the High Priest of the new covenant, opened a new path that provides direct access into God's very throne room.[7] This new relationship with God has a more intimate quality. God's law is not written on tables of stone, but in our very hearts, changing us from the inside out.[8] The salvation of the new covenant establishes a relationship with God that takes the meaning of the "people of God" up to a new level. In Hebrews, believers become the "house of God."[9] The work of Christ in salvation brings us into a new family relationship with God as sons and daughters.[10]

Salvation in Christ also establishes a relationship with God that allows us to gain knowledge of God by direct relationship with him. Our knowledge of God is no longer mediated through a prophet, priest, or king as in the old covenant.[11] The Holy Spirit, our helper, has come to live inside us and helps us to know God.[12] Finally, the new covenant replaces fear to draw near to God with confidence to come into his presence. The permanent removal of sin by the sacrifice of Jesus gives us confidence to enter God's presence. Salvation in the new covenant gives us a whole new relationship with God that places us in the very throne room of God in worship and relationship.

THE BEAUTY OF SALVATION

Salvation doesn't only remove something from us; it also gives something to us, and what it gives us is not just for later. We've just seen that Jesus gives us a new relationship with God that grants us access to the Lord's presence now in prayer and worship. The Lord himself is the pinnacle of beauty. When we worship God, the perfection of his presence shines into the cracks of our lives, bringing hope into brokenness. But beyond access to gaze on the beauty of God, salvation does something else for us that is more personal; salvation makes us beautiful. The psalmist says, "For the LORD taketh pleasure in his people: he will beautify the meek with salvation."[13] It is those who are humble and broken before him that God will bless with salvation.[14]

Another form of this word "beautify" is used in Isaiah 61:3 and illuminates a striking meaning.[15] The verse says the Messiah will give those who mourn in Zion a crown of beauty instead of ashes.[16] Isaiah is saying that ashes on the head of God's people will be replaced by a beautiful crown one day. Salvation makes us beautiful because it changes our identity. We who were the enemies of God[17] are given a new identity as sons and daughters of God Most High. Our new identity is not only being children of God but also becoming those who will inherit God's kingdom and reign with him on earth.[18]

We see another picture of the beauty of salvation in the old covenant description of the priests' clothing: "May your priests be clothed with righteousness," and "I will clothe her priests with salvation."[19] In Scripture clothing can have a meaning that is both symbolic and substantive. When Adam and Eve sinned against God, he slew an animal and took the skins and made garments to cover their nakedness and shame. This gives us a picture of salvation in the garments God made for Adam and Eve by a sacrifice. The garments also served the practical use of covering their shame and nakedness.[20] Pharaoh placed a robe of glory on Joseph to signify his promotion to serve next to the throne of Egypt beside Pharaoh himself.[21] Mordecai wore a royal robe when he was honored before the king after exposing an assassination plot.[22] There is also the negative sense—the consequence of not having the proper clothing. In the parable of the wedding feast, Jesus says that a man who did not have on the proper clothing for the feast was bound and cast out.[23] Not having the proper garments can have disastrous results.

For a person who wants to draw near to God, salvation is essential clothing. Salvation means deliverance from sin and its consequences into a new quality of life that is eternal and blessed. Salvation can be described as both deliverance "from" and deliverance "to." Salvation is deliverance from the penalty of sin (death),[24] the power of sin (to reign in our bodies),[25] and presence of sin (its existence in our bodies).[26] Salvation is deliverance into a new identity (sonship),[27] a new relationship (in a new covenant),[28] a new reality (the kingdom of God),[29] and a new inheritance (new destiny—heaven)[30] in Jesus Christ. Salvation is the gift of God in Jesus Christ that serves as the very clothing that we wear in relationship with God.

One of the blessings of salvation is that God robes us with his righteousness. If we had to stand before God in our own righteousness, we would be ashamed and in trouble. Isaiah reminds us that the very righteous deeds we do are as filthy rags to God.[31] This is not saying that our righteous deeds have no value with God. It is saying that our righteous deeds—compared to the righteousness of God—are like filthy rags, and filthy rags will never gain us acceptance with God. For us to be acceptable to God, he had to find a way to make us righteous. Paul points out how he did it in 2 Corinthians 5:21: "God made him who had no sin to be sin for us, so that in him we might become the righteousness of God."

Jesus not only removed the stain of sin from us, but he also robed us in his righteousness so that we, like priests, would stand before God with a robe of beauty appropriate for God's presence. Through Jesus we fulfill the Old Testament hope that the priests of God would be clothed with righteousness.[32] The righteousness of God is the perfect standard of what is right and true, and the standard is God himself.[33] Righteousness is all that conforms to the good, acceptable, and perfect will of

God. The righteousness of God makes us beautiful. It changes our identity from being enemies of God to being his sons and daughters with heaven as our new home. It changes our reality from the decaying ugliness of sin and death to the recreative beauty of righteousness and life.

When we stand clothed in the righteousness of God, we stand with dignity, glory, and beauty because we bear his image.[34] We don't have to fear coming into his presence; we now bear the very righteousness of God in ourselves because of the sacrifice of Jesus. The clothing of the priests set them apart for service in the sanctuary of God and designated them as those who were able to draw near to him. Exodus tells us that the garments of Aaron and his sons were for "glory and . . . beauty."[35] To work in such close proximity to God, the priests' clothing needed to reflect God's glory and beauty. Their clothing made them presentable before God.

The salvation of the new covenant establishes us in a new relationship with God as priests who are clothed in the righteousness of God, which makes us both glorious and beautiful to our heavenly Father. Salvation changes what is true about us. The perfect sacrifice of Jesus Christ provides a salvation that transforms us from the inside out, uniquely clothing us with the glory and beauty that make us fit to enter the very presence of God. Salvation doesn't just free us from the penalty of sin, it gives us direct access to the throne room of God Almighty now.

When I am in need in this present world, I don't have to wait for heaven; I can come boldly into the throne room of God to find the grace and mercy to help. Salvation makes possible a different way of life. I am never alone. I can come into God's presence in prayer and bask in his beauty anytime and anywhere. I am never without hope. Even in the desperation of the desert when I'm about to give out, I can come to God's throne. And when I do, I enter a new, heavenly realm where a whole different range of possibilities exist and the biggest hindrance to experiencing them is my faith. Salvation makes possible a way of life where, clothed in the righteousness and beauty of Christ, we can confidently enter God's presence as a part of normal life.

CHAPTER 12

THE COMMUNITY of TRUE WORSHIP

MY TWO-AND-A-HALF-YEAR STINT in Moscow was the first time in my life I had lived outside of my own country. From this new vantage point, I could look back on my experience of life in America with a fresh objectivity, especially with the help of some of my Russian and Ukrainian friends. I realized how individualistic our society is. Now, that's not all bad. Individuality is important, and there are weaknesses in societies that are very community-centered in their orientation. But there are also strengths. In Russia, for example, there was a much stronger sense of connectedness between people in community than I experienced in America. Historically, this stems from the need to depend on one another to survive in the harsh climate of the region. But I saw how easy it is in the United States to focus on individual rights, freedoms, and needs to the extent that I lose sight of the needs of others, and my need of them. TV commercials and Internet ads constantly bombard us with reminders of our individual needs, and why we can't live without certain products and services. It is as if I can seal myself off from the world around me and depend on technology to bring me everything I need.

But reality is different. God created us incomplete for a reason. He made us with the need for air, water, and food, or we die. Also, it is impossible to grow, mature, and live a healthy, whole human life without the love, affirmation, and attention of others. Other people help provide what we lack and help fill the areas of our lives that are incomplete. This is true with our devotional life as well. Devotional life is not only a private, individual exercise but also a corporate experience of believers together. It is not only meeting God alone in the secret place of his presence, it is also meeting him in the midst of his people when they gather. None of us has all he or she needs to fully worship and seek God alone. While the quietness of a time alone with God is a marvelous experience of worship, we encounter a completely different reality when we come before God's presence with a group of people. The possibilities are different precisely because of the multitude of individuals with different personalities, experiences, and depths of relationship with God (and some are probably not believers).

We said that our devotional life engages our entire inner life in an unceasing relationship with the God of creation and redemption in all of life. Whether prayer, worship, artistic expression, Bible reading, meditation and study, obedience, word, or action, none of these forms of devotional life will be adequate to fully experience God unless we also engage in them with others. In reading, meditation, and study, we will always be helped by the insights, understanding, and correction we receive from other believers as we delve into God's Word. When we pray, it's important to remember that Jesus himself said, "Again, I tell you that if two of you on earth agree about anything you ask for, it will be done for you by my Father in heaven. For where two or three come together in my name, there am I with them."[1] While in my heart I might be committed to obeying God, I can also be blinded to an area of sin in my life that someone else can see and help me address.[2] Whether painting, playing music, or whatever my form of artistic expression, it will need the help of others to develop so that I can contribute what I am truly capable of. When we experience a desert season in life, one of the most natural responses is to isolate ourselves from others. That was easy for me to do six thousand miles from home in an apartment alone in the largest city in Russia. I just wanted to avoid other people who may have misunderstood me or added to the pain. And a little self-pity felt good when I was hurting! At other times I felt, "I'm hurting, just leave me alone." But God's Word began to well up inside me. It reminded me that one of the biggest strategies of the wolf is to separate a lamb from the flock. A sheep is much easier prey when it's alone. Ecclesiastes says, "Two are better than one, because they have a good return for their work: If one falls down, his friend can help him up. But pity the man who falls and has no one to help him up!"[3] Instead of withdrawing from my community of friends, it was going to them that helped me discover what God was saying to me and how I could connect with him to find the strength and understanding I needed to make it through the desert.

Both the Old and New Testaments point out two things that help us see the importance of community in worship and devotional life. First, throughout Scripture we see that God manifests his presence in the midst of the community of his people. Second, both Testaments make it clear that true worship extends beyond the prayer closet to the gatherings of God's people for worship and relationship with one another in community. Let's take a journey through Scripture to see how these two themes unfold.

THE EXODUS TO KING DAVID

The theme of God's unique dwelling in his people as a community is evident from the final days of Israel's bondage to Egypt forward. When God caused gnats to cover Egypt they were everywhere, except Goshen where Israel lived.[4] When God sent boils on the people, it afflicted only the Egyptians.[5] Strangely, the hail[6] and the darkness[7] fell only on the Egyptians, leaving Israel free from hail and darkness. Finally, God instituted the Passover in an unforgettable act of judgment, killing the first-born of every Egyptian family, human and animal, but the people of God suffered no loss. They sprinkled the blood of the Passover lamb over their doorposts, causing the judgment of God to "pass over" them. It wasn't only with these events that God displayed his unique presence with his people; in the journey from Egypt, the cloud by day and the pillar of fire by night guided them.[8] In fact the cloud, along with the Angel of God, came in front of the Egyptian army, blocking them from harming Israel when God's people were against the Red Sea.[9]

During the forty years of wandering, God's presence hovered over the tabernacle in the cloud by day and a pillar of fire by night. When it was time for the people to move to a new location, the cloud or the fire would move, and the people would break camp and follow it.[10] During this time, the tabernacle was the center of the camp[11] and the center of the worship life of the nation. God was present in a visible and unique manner in the midst of his people at the tabernacle.[12]

During the period of the judges until early in the reign of King David, the tabernacle was located primarily at Shiloh,[13] which is where the community experienced God's presence.[14] It is more difficult to determine the location of the tabernacle during the reigns of King David and King Solomon,[15] except that the book of 1 Chronicles tells us it was at Gibeon during much of this time.[16] It is significant that David, knowing the ark of the covenant symbolized the throne of God in heaven and served as his throne on earth,[17] brought the ark to Jerusalem after he conquered it and placed the ark in a tent.[18] This was the first step in establishing Jerusalem as the center of worship and brought the presence of God, with the ark of the covenant, to dwell in the City of David.

FROM THE FIRST TEMPLE TO THE SECOND

While David set the conditions for Jerusalem to be the center of worship for Israel, it was Solomon who built and dedicated the temple in Jerusalem. When Solomon finished his prayer of dedication over the temple, fire from God came down from heaven and consumed the offerings and sacrifices, and the presence of God filled the temple with such glory that the priests had to leave it.[19] These two extraordinary events answered once and for all the question of where God placed his presence in the nation of Israel. The temple was the dwelling place of God on earth[20] and the spiritual center of the nation of Israel. God also appeared to Solomon during this time to confirm his presence in the temple, saying that he would put his name in the temple.[21]

After Solomon, the nation of Israel split in two, forming a northern kingdom (Israel) and a southern kingdom (Judah). Idolatry grew like a virus in Israel and Judah in the permissive environments created by many of Judah's and Israel's kings, who were wicked. During this time, their increasing appetite for idolatry eventually led them both into captivity.[22] The northern kingdom, Israel, was taken captive to Assyria in 721 BC.[23] Judah was not far behind, being taken captive to Babylon in 587 BC.[24]

In the Babylonian exile, we find a fascinating story of hope in how God met his people in captivity. In the book of Ezekiel, written during the exile in Babylon, God said to his people that even though he sent them into captivity, "Yet for a little while I have been a sanctuary for them in the countries where they have gone."[25] While God's people were under his harsh discipline for their unfaithfulness to his covenant and idolatry, he was present in their midst in the very countries they were held. In Ezekiel, God expressed his displeasure with his people through a vision of God's glory departing from the temple. God's glory, the visible manifestation of his presence in the midst of his people, departed leaving it an empty shell.[26] The temple had become little more than a charm for good fortune, a lifeless shrine. The people placed their faith in it but did not follow God.[27] In the vision, God was showing his people how he responded to their persistent unfaithfulness: He left. God withdrew his presence from the temple and sent the armies of Nebuchadnezzar to rob the temple of its treasure and leave it in burned ruins.

God is a magnificent and holy God. He will not allow his people to use him like a genie in a bottle to be summoned when they want something, while disregarding their relationship with him. He didn't leave them without hope, though, and in another vision he told them that one day the glory of God would return to the temple and fill it; and in that day, his people would no longer run after lifeless idols, but serve him alone.[28]

In the closing period of the Old Testament, Judah returned from bondage in Babylon, and under the leadership of the priest, the prophets and the governor rebuilt the temple.[29] God promised the people that the glory of this house would surpass the glory of Solomon's temple.[30] Despite the diminished physical presence of the second temple,[31] God was nonetheless in the midst of his people again, and the stage was set for a whole new order with the coming of the High Priest of the new covenant.

But before we go to the New Testament, we need to look more carefully at the message of the Old Testament prophets. The detestable idolatry of this period inflamed the prophets of God. In their scathing rebukes against the people of Israel lay an important clarification of what true worship of God means.

A CLOSER LOOK AT WORSHIP IN THE OLD TESTAMENT

In the period of Israel's history between Solomon's reign and the Exile, the people were confused. They assumed that because God placed his name on the temple, all they had to do was associate themselves with the temple and they would be safe. They felt no personal responsibility to God for the spiritual quality of their lives or the impact of their lives on others. The people concluded that they could live however they wanted, with no regard for what God had revealed about his desires for them. And then they could come to the temple and worship as if God were pleased with them. Incidentally, we see this same attitude today. It's the belief that we can "respectfully" disregard God's Word and then come into the sanctuary of a church and expect God's favor to be on us, simply because we associate ourselves with a place where God is present.

God's message is that the people who are called by his name should associate themselves with him by how they live, not where they sing worship songs and do religious service once or twice a week. A life associated with God is one that reflects those things that God values. Corporately, devotional life means spending regular time together with God's people in God's presence, not so that we can be entertained but so that we will become more like the One we are worshipping. This only makes sense because at the core of worship is deep admiration. So let's see how the prophets unveil the picture of true worship.

Isaiah begins his book with a sharp rebuke of God's people, calling them a nation with the character of Sodom and Gomorrah.[32] He goes on to say that their offerings and other acts of religious service to God are worthless and meaningless because of the way they are treating others in the community.[33] From social wrongs, such as failing to provide justice for widows and orphans, to murder, God's people did not treat each other with the mercy, love, righteousness, and justice he desired of them. Isaiah's message was that if their lives were characterized by this kind of wrongdoing, they shouldn't bother coming to God for worship.

Later, in Isaiah 58, the prophet once again lays a searing accusation on the people of Judah. He says that they were going through motions of worship, namely fasting, while their lives and their manner of treating one another dishonored God. His message to them was simple: True worship must impact the way we live and treat one another. Isaiah claimed that even their spiritual activities resulted in arguments and fights.[34] He said that their worship was not just insincere, but hypocritical. They went through the motions of being contrite and humble, but their hearts were far from God: "These people come near to me with their mouth and honor me with their lips, but their hearts are far from me."[35]

Isaiah rebuked the nation because they were oppressing their own people, probably in an unjust system of slavery.[36] Breaking the yoke is an image of completely destroying "the means of oppression."[37] Isaiah is saying that when the community's worship is genuine, it produces acts of compassion and love for others and of intolerance for injustice and oppression. It is interesting that when he describes positively the life that genuinely worships God, he emphasizes serving the marginalized: the poor, the homeless, the naked, and those in need.[38] Isaiah also denounces "pointing [the] finger,"[39] an action that disrespects and dishonors another person,[40] and using words that are hurtful to others.[41] In summary, God's people experience him in community when they reflect his character in how they relate to each other, and because of it, he is present in their midst.

The prophet Micah brings a similar charge against Israel, asking them what kind of worship God desires.[42] He gives a threefold answer. First, the kind of "sacrifice" that God desires of us is to act with justice toward others. When we consider that the foundation of God's throne in heaven is righteousness and justice,[43] we can see how appropriate it is that doing acts of justice for others is an act of worshipping God. Second, to worship God is to love mercy. The big idea in the word *mercy* here, חֶסֶד (kheh·sed), is kindness shown toward people, but especially to those who are most vulnerable, those in misery, those in need.[44] God is a God of mercy,[45] and those who worship him will reflect his mercy to those around them. Finally, Micah says that a true worshipper walks humbly with God. The word *walk*, הָלַךְ (haw·lak), is a general word for walk that often means simply to live.[46] To walk with God means to live every aspect of life in the awareness of God's presence and with the intent to please him in thought, word, and deed. To walk "humbly" with God means that in my daily life the spirit in which I relate to God is one of reverent respect and trust. When I deeply respect someone, I behave in his or her presence according to the "weight" of his or her person. The word for God's "glory" in Hebrew is the word *kaw·bode*, meaning "heavy." Humility understands the weight of God's glory and honors him above everything and everyone else. Humility that is genuine always leads to trust. To walk humbly with God means that I will trust God and submit myself to him even when I don't understand the hard twists of life.

The Old Testament prophets leave us with a picture of worship that is beyond people gathering to sing hymns, pray prayers, hear a sermon, and celebrate other important parts of worship, as essential as these things are. Their concept of worship reaches into the everyday life of the community of God's people and looks at how we care for the most vulnerable among us. The New Testament authors pick up the idea of worship where the Old Testament prophets leave off, and the sanctuary imagery figures prominently in it.

THE NEW TEMPLE OF GOD

Earlier in the chapter, we pointed out two distinct ways the corporate nature of worship appears in the Old Testament: (1) God manifests his presence in the midst of the community of his people, and (2) true worship extends beyond gatherings of people to include the way they relate to one another in community. The new covenant in the blood of Jesus Christ and the coming of the Holy Spirit take these two big themes from the Old Testament to a whole new level.

Jesus told the Eleven that when he left them he would not leave them in the world alone. He promised to send the Holy Spirit, and that the Holy Spirit would not only be with them but also in them.[47] At Pentecost, the Holy Spirit came upon the apostles and then began to come upon both Jewish and Gentile believers, showing that God was indeed bringing the blessings of his salvation into the nations of the world. As the gospel began to grow in areas like the city of Corinth in southern Greece, communities of believers began to form. Even though the apostle Paul addresses the believers in Corinth as spiritually immature "infants,"[48] he encourages them with the news that they, together, were a temple of God.[49] He further explains that the very Spirit of God himself dwelt among them, just as God dwelt in the tabernacle and temple of the Old Testament.

The Holy Spirit dwells in the community of believers, making them the dwelling place of God, his temple. This means that God is present, not in a building of stone, wood, and gold, but in a living, moving "temple" of people who rub shoulders with each other. The temple of

God is no longer confined to one location, but is now mobile, bringing the presence of God in touch with the world. Paul repeats this theme in 2 Corinthians, this time including himself with them: "For we are the temple of the living God."[50] Paul explains that this means God will live and walk among them.

This reality can change how we do life! God is present in the midst of his people while they walk, ride, and drive their way through life. The question is: Are we in touch with this reality, or are we disconnected from it? Is God calling but our phone is turned off because we are too busy doing life? He is there in our midst and we miss him. Remember, Jesus said that where two or three believers are together in his name, he is with them.[51] In the New Testament God moves into the neighborhood and lives among his people, extending his grace and truth to the world through them.[52]

In Ephesians 2, Paul also describes God's people in community as "a holy temple in the Lord." He goes on to say, "And in him you, too, are being built together to become a dwelling in which God lives by his Spirit."[53] Now, to the church in Ephesus and to the surrounding churches of western Asia Minor,[54] Paul teaches that those who were totally outside of God's chosen people, Israel, have now been brought near by the sacrifice of Jesus. He says that now they are not only "fellow citizens with God's people and members of God's household"[55] but also "a holy temple in the Lord. And in him . . . are being built together to become a dwelling in which God lives by his Spirit."[56] Non-Jewish peoples are now members of God's household and become a holy temple where the Holy Spirit lives. We in the new covenant are a holy temple, the dwelling place of God by his Holy Spirit. This is true individually,[57] as a community,[58] and as the universal church of Jesus.[59]

It is not my intent here to suggest that buildings cannot be spaces where God is present in a special way. It is beyond the purpose of this book to explore the subject of "sacred space" and its role in our worship life. Instead, I wish to call attention to this message of the biblical authors that in the New Testament the people of God become his dwelling place, his temple.

WORSHIP IN THE NEW TESTAMENT

The New Testament authors expand the understanding and practice of worship beyond precincts of the temple into everyday life. We may begin with Jesus himself, who said that if a person is at the temple offering a sacrifice and remembers that he has a conflict with someone, he must leave his offering at the altar. First, the person must be reconciled to his "brother" or "sister," and then come and offer his gift.[60] Jesus' words here announce that worship includes attention to relationships in our lives. How we handle offenses and forgiveness[61] are a matter of worship and relationship with God. This is why the apostle John says that if we do not love our brother whom we have seen, we cannot love God whom we have not seen.[62] Our worship of God is interwoven with the relationships in our lives. We cannot do one without the other.

Paul refers to giving financially with terms of worship. In Romans 15, he uses one of the New Testament words for worship — λειτουργέω (li·toorg·eh·o) — to describe the monetary gift the non-Jewish churches shared with the poor believers in Jerusalem.[63] Speaking of the financial gift that Epaphroditus brought to Paul from the Philippians, Paul calls his effort bringing the gift a λειτουργία (li·toorg·ee·ah) (service of worship).[64] He later speaks of the gift as "a fragrant offering, an acceptable sacrifice pleasing to God."[65] This language is from the sacrifices at the tabernacle and brings the act of giving into the realm of worship.

Finally, in the book of Hebrews the author exhorts his audience to worship God as an expression of gratitude for the unshakable kingdom they are receiving. He then begins chapter 13 by listing six specific services of worship his readers could adopt.[66] Later in the chapter, he writes: "And do not forget to do good and to share with others, for with such sacrifices God is pleased."[67] The book of Hebrews applies the language of worship (sacrifices)[68] to doing good and sharing with others.

Hebrews sees doing good and sharing with others as acceptable sacrifices of worship we offer to God.

Our devotional life is not only for the closet; it is for the street. Worship doesn't include only certain activities in a church building on a certain day of the week. Worship means reflecting the character of God into the relationships and communities where we live. Are we offering God acceptable worship? Have we so individualized worship that we have missed the power of being the dwelling place of God on a city block, in an office, in a community? It's time to recover the power of what it means to be the dwelling place of God as a people in the world. And it's time to extend our worship out to where it belongs, not confined to our churches and community gatherings but bursting into the whole of life.

CHAPTER 13

TRANSFORMATION from the INSIDE OUT

WHEN I LANDED in Moscow the first time, it was January and the whole world was frozen. I looked out the plane window and saw a baggage handler grimacing in the biting cold, with icicles hanging from his mustache. I said to myself, *Hello, this is not Texas!* As I considered my new world, I had a sinking feeling: "What do the people of Russia need, and why would they want what we are offering them?" I had walked with God for twenty years, but now I was in a very different world. Was God really here? What was he doing?

As I spent time with God in my Moscow flat, I began to see that my picture of devotional life was deficient. I needed more than just a private prayer closet that would help me maintain my personal relationship with God; I needed a connection into the main line of the God of the universe who had been active in Russia long before I was born. I didn't have a clue what to do or where to start. My idea of devotional life was about to collide with reality.

To what kind of devotional life does the sanctuary imagery of Scripture point? Is it only to focus our attention upward, toward God, and inward, toward our own inner person? Does it lead us to look only into our own communities of faith? Can our worship of God, if it is authentic and whole, have only a private and community focus? In this final chapter, we will look at devotional life not only as an individual or community experience but also as an extension of my inner spiritual life into God's mission in the world. To see the connection between worship and mission more clearly, we are going to take a look at both ideas and explore how they relate. Let's start with worship.

THE HEART OF WORSHIP

We've looked at worship in detail in chapters 5 and 6, so here we only want to summarize our earlier conversations by saying that at the heart of worship are two things: adoration and service. Adoration means paying honor to God in a manner that expresses his worth.[1] What does it mean to honor God? We could take a poll and come up with some great ideas about honoring God. But what does God say it takes to honor him? One of the clearest themes in Scripture can be seen in Isaiah 29:13 where we read, "The Lord says: 'These people come near to me with their mouth and honor me with their lips, but their hearts are far from me. Their worship of me is made up only of rules taught by men.'"

God is not pleased with our adoration when we honor him with our words and religious services, but our hearts are far from him. Honoring God begins in the heart. In our inner life, where we make choices, God wants us to honor him by choosing to put him first. Our inner life is a gift from God. We may do with it what we choose, and we will give account to God for our choice. Our outer lives are an overflow of our inner lives. God wants to be honored in our inner world, where the choices of life are made. Putting it another way, to honor God is to honor his Word and his will by obeying them. Many passages in Scripture teach that to honor God means to obey him.[2] We honor God by placing value on what he says is important, not only in word but with our attitudes and actions as well.

Service is also at the heart of worship. Remember that the Hebrew verb (aw·bad), "to serve," also means to work and to worship. In

Deuteronomy, Moses uses this word to describe how God desires his people to live, showing allegiance to him in every area of life.[3] Serving God means living a life that honors God's will, his Word, and his commands. Jesus demonstrated the core meaning of worship in his response to the Devil when he was tempted in the desert. Satan offered Jesus the kingdoms of the world if he would bow down and worship him. When Jesus tells him we are to worship and serve only God, he is affirming that our submission, loyalty, and service are to God alone.[4]

GOD AT WORK IN THE WORLD

What is God doing in the world? What is God doing in Russia? I thought of that often sitting at my kitchen window staring out at row after row of twenty-story apartment buildings as far as I could see in southwest Moscow. Is there a grand plan God is carrying out in the world; if there is, can I join him? The answer to that is a resounding yes. God is at work in the world advancing his kingdom against the kingdom of darkness, and he invites us to join him.[5]

God's people have a choice. We can join him in the mission of expanding his kingdom or be only spectators who watch the wave of God's transforming power sweep through families, communities, and nations. We can join God in many ways, but we will describe four big movements that contribute to the expansion of his kingdom in the world.

The first is simple and powerful: how people live. In first-century Thessalonica, the followers of Jesus led such vibrant lives that their reputation spread throughout central and southern Greece and beyond.[6] The kingdom of God advances through the impact of people whose everyday lives give off the fragrance of Jesus and his kingdom. These are people who live as if their daily lives are offerings to God, just like the offerings at the bronze altar. Living is not acting; it is an outward expression of an inner life with Jesus. In the Beatitudes, Jesus revealed what kind of outer life the kingdom of God produces when it is at work in the inner life:

- Treating others with kindness, Matthew 5:5,7
- Making peace where conflict exists, Matthew 5:9
- Displaying grace instead of anger, Matthew 5:21-22
- Forgiving the unforgivable, Matthew 6:14-15
- Generously helping those in need, Luke 6:30
- Loving a person's enemies, Luke 6:27-29

The tabernacle points us to a relationship with God that connects our inner life with the power and reality of the King and his kingdom. As the influence of the kingdom grows in a person's inner life, it transforms him or her from the inside out. We don't have to act differently; we become people who are different. The kingdom of God expands like leaven[7] because people notice real change and it is attractive. Real change happens from the inside out.

Second, the kingdom grows through the storytelling of ordinary people in whom Jesus lives. In Scripture this is called "bearing witness,"[8] and it means to share our experience of Jesus with the people in our lives. A person who is a witness has personal experience that qualifies him or her to "give testimony," as in a courtroom. A rich devotional life means that we experience God in the day-to-day ebb and flow of life, and because of this we have something to share. God is present with us and we are present with him in everyday life, seeing his hand at work and enjoying him. Bearing witness simply means sharing those stories.

A third movement of the kingdom is through the preaching of the Word of the gospel.[9] The postmodern and post-Christian culture in many first- and second-world countries will require creative and diverse means of preaching the Word. But declaring the truth and grace of the message of Jesus and his kingdom publicly will always be a significant way the kingdom advances.

Finally, disciple making expands the kingdom of God. Before Jesus left the world, he commanded the Eleven to go make disciples of all nations.[10] They understood what he meant because he did it with them. We are speaking of a movement that molds the next generation life-on-life as Jesus did with the Twelve. Disciple making focuses on forming Christ in the lives of those who enter the kingdom.[11] It also produces followers of Jesus who are capable of reproducing themselves spiritually in the lives of the next generation.[12]

No part of the process of discipling is more important than helping the next generation develop a deep and healthy devotional life. The book of Psalms says that one generation should declare the praiseworthy deeds of God to the next and that this pattern should be continued generation after generation.[13] In disciple making this means helping the new disciple of Jesus step into a real and vibrant relationship with God. It means teaching others how to connect with God, how to worship him, and how to know him, by doing it with them. Disciple making helps establish the new believer in a devotional life that keeps him or her in vital communion with God in every aspect of life. So, disciple making extends the kingdom of God because it produces a movement of people alive with the reality of God, men and women who are capable of reproducing themselves spiritually in subsequent generations.

WORSHIP AND MISSION

How then are worship and mission related? Is there a connection between our life of worship and the mission of God's kingdom in the world? To answer these questions we begin in God himself. One quality of God's character that gives us insight into the relationship between worship and mission is the integrity of God. To speak of the integrity of God is to say that God is perfectly consistent throughout every area of his being. There is no inconsistency or discrepancy in God. We see the integrity of God in his truth. In the Old Testament the Hebrew word *eh·meth* is the word most often translated "truth" or "faithfulness."

This word means that which is faithful, consistent, or loyal, and says that God is consistent with his true character in everything he does.

Integrity is also an aspect of the righteousness of God. His righteousness is the standard of what is right and true. God is righteous in all his ways, and everything he does conforms to his standard of what is right (Psalm 145:17; Daniel 9:14). His holiness also carries the idea of integrity. God is holy; there is nothing unholy or imperfect in him. He is the same, holy, throughout all he is and all he does. God is the same throughout; he is perfectly consistent in all that he is. His words, his ideas, his will, and his truth are consistent throughout. There is no discrepancy or inconsistency in God.

God expects the same of us who are created in his image. He says, for example, that we should be holy because he is holy.[14] We cannot praise God with our mouths when our actions contradict the very words of our prayers and songs. True worship of God is reflected in how we live and what we do. God is a God of integrity; his actions perfectly reflect his character. His people, also, should be a people of integrity whose lives are consistent with the character of God from the inside out. As we saw in the previous section, when our life of worship permeates all we do, our simple acts of love and obedience to God in everyday life extend the kingdom of God. By worshipping God in the whole of life, we are engaged in his mission right where we live.

I always enjoyed the five-hour bus ride from Moscow to Vladimir. The massive power lines that crisscrossed the Russian countryside intrigued me as I peered out the ice-crusted windows. These huge structures carried power to the villages that dotted the Russian steppe. This cozy scene helps me think about the importance of integrity in worship and mission from the example of the power line. If the wire of a power line is not properly insulated, the power cannot flow through it without being shorted out. A life of integrity is like the insulation around a wire that allows the power to flow along the wire to its destination. When the insulation around the wire has "integrity," it is whole, not broken or inconsistent, and the power can flow through the wire with its full potency. When holiness, righteousness, and truth clothe our inner life and shape our outer life, we have the insulation needed to turn on the power and presence of God so that it can flow through our lives.

WORSHIP AND MISSION IN THE OLD TESTAMENT

In chapter 12 we saw how the Old Testament prophets Isaiah, Hosea, Joel, Amos, Micah, and Malachi chastised God's people because there was a lack of integrity between their worship and their lives. Living is missional. When a person's daily behavior, habits, and actions are in sync with Jesus, his or her life engages the world with the values and message of the kingdom. As Hosea says, "I desire mercy, not sacrifice, and acknowledgment of God rather than burnt offerings."[15] The sacrifice God wanted was the people themselves. Later, the apostle Paul writes that believers should present their bodies as living sacrifices to God.[16] The believer's whole life is to be a sacrifice to God.

After asking what kind of sacrifices (worship) God desires, Micah highlights not only walking humbly with God but says that the Lord requires his people "to act justly and to love mercy."[17] Acting justly is something a person does. Worshipping God is doing what is right in the circumstances of our lives.[18] The idea of justice also includes making right something that is wrong. Micah makes it clear that true worship means offering God acts of justice as sacrifices that please him. As we offer God these acts of worship, we are joining God in the work of extending his rule and reign into the world — a place where people are mistreated and hurt by others, and where power is often used for evil and not good.

Hosea and Micah both mention mercy. God did not desire the outward show of animal sacrifices, but the outward display of love coming from a heart full of mercy. The word translated *mercy* here means goodness and kindness, especially shown toward those in need or misery.[19] Instead of his people taking advantage of the weak or vulnerable, God expected them to show kindness and compassion to others, providing the support they needed.

WORSHIP AND MISSION IN THE NEW TESTAMENT

The New Testament authors use the language of worship in ways that expand our understanding of worship to include an outward missional dimension. In describing his calling, Paul says that God gave him grace to be "a minister of Christ Jesus to the Gentiles with the priestly duty of proclaiming the gospel of God, so that the Gentiles might become an offering acceptable to God."[20] Paul uses imagery from the worship life of the sanctuary to express his calling. He says that proclaiming the gospel to the non-Jewish world was his priestly service to God.[21] The result of Paul's priestly ministry is that the Gentiles who believe become an offering to God.[22] This is what Paul had just urged his audience to do earlier in the epistle, to present their bodies, that is their whole lives, as a living sacrifice to God.[23] Paul uses the language of worship in Romans 15 in a way that expands its meaning to include preaching the gospel.[24]

We find a similar expression in another of Paul's letters where he calls the life of the Philippian community an acceptable offering to God. He says, "But even if I am being poured out like a drink offering on the sacrifice and service coming from your faith, I am glad and rejoice with all of you."[25] The language in this verse again takes full advantage of the sanctuary imagery of sacrifice. These believers had such faith that their lives were a sacrifice and service to God.[26] The apostle expresses the extent to which he is willing to go to see this quality of life produced in the Philippians. Just as drink offerings were poured out at the foot of the bronze altar,[27] Paul is willing to be poured out if it means maturity and fruitfulness in the lives of God's people there.[28] Paul again extends the language of worship into the territory of mission. The hard and often painful labor involved in bringing the gospel to people is an offering poured out in service to God.

In the closing chapter of the book of Hebrews, the author refers to doing good and sharing with others as sacrifices that are pleasing to God.[29] This statement places doing good and sharing with others under the heading of worship. One way to share is giving financially to help others. In the writings of Paul, giving to the poor is considered an offering and a service of worship to God.[30] The apostle James says that pure religion or worship[31] means taking care of the vulnerable, specifically orphans and widows. And Jesus himself exhorts his followers to allow others to see the light of their good works so that they may one day bring glory to God.[32]

GOD'S PRESENCE, GOD'S SANCTUARY, AND CONQUEST

One of the most unique conversations in the Bible occurs between Moses and God in the book of Exodus. Moses is reminding the Lord that the Israelites are his people and that he can't lead the people in his own power. God interrupts Moses' complaint. He promises that his presence will go with Moses and that he will give him peace.[33] God's presence in the midst of his people in the tabernacle and temple was not only for their joy and blessing but also for victory in battle. God promised to give his people the land of Canaan as their inheritance,[34] but they had to conquer it. God now promised Moses that his presence would go with Israel as they went to take the Promised Land. When Israel came to Jericho to begin the conquest of the land, Rahab told the two spies that the hearts of the people of Jericho had melted in fear of Israel because they had heard that God's power was with Israel. They heard that God parted the Red Sea and helped Israel defeat two Amorite kings.[35] It was in the power of God that Israel eventually conquered most of the Promised Land.[36] But that is not the greatest conquest God and his people will achieve.

In the second psalm, God, who is enthroned in heaven,[37] installs his Son as King on Zion. This psalm is often quoted in the New

Testament[38] and is a messianic psalm pointing to Jesus as the Messiah, the coming King.[39] In this psalm, God invites the Son to ask him for the nations as an inheritance.[40] As we have seen, God is bringing salvation to the nations as he promised Abraham.[41] Jesus, the Messiah, is fulfilling this by bringing many sons and daughters to glory from every nation.[42] But how is Jesus accomplishing that since he is no longer on earth but in heaven? He is present in his people as a living temple[43] and is at work in the world through their lives as they extend the love, grace, and truth of God to those around them. This is living out a life of holistic worship. The kingdom of God advances through Christ's body on earth and is empowered by his Spirit who lives in them. Conquest in the new covenant is not by the weapons of warfare but by the power of grace and truth in the person of Jesus Christ, the Messiah.

WORSHIP, MISSION, AND THE NATIONS

The journey of knowing God takes us into the very heart of God himself. As we come to know God more fully, one thing we notice is his desire for the nations. From the first mention of the gospel in Genesis 12, God is concerned with bringing the blessings of his kingdom to all the nations of the world.[44] In the book of Psalms, a major theme of God's desire for the nations emerges: God wants the nations to worship him. Psalm 22 says, "All the families of the nations will bow down before him."[45] It is not surprising, then, that the temple is called a house of prayer for all nations.[46] God welcomes all the nations to come before him to worship and celebrate his splendor and majesty. The beauty and glory of God are not for one individual or one people, but for all nations, which are shaped by God's hand.[47] And in the end times, we will see the nations of the world gathered to worship God himself in the New Jerusalem, which will have no temple in it because the Lord himself will be its sanctuary.[48]

THE DESERT, DEVOTIONAL LIFE, AND MISSION

The desert is a place of formation and preparation for mission and destiny. Israel spent forty years in the desert[49] before beginning the conquest of the Promised Land. Israel was not ready to go from bondage to conquest.[50] During the years in the desert, God forged a mighty army from this wandering horde. The pain and testing of the desert prepared them to trust God with the ever-present threats of life and death in war. Following four decades of discipline, Israel marched into Canaan and claimed the Promised Land from the hands of many ungodly nations.

On a far grander scale, Jesus also went into the desert for forty days of fasting before beginning his public ministry. From Christ's time in the desert, Luke says that he emerged full of the Holy Spirit and power. And in that power he fulfilled his mission and destiny to redeem humanity from the dominion of sin, death, and the Devil. Whether our desert experiences are days, weeks, months, or years in length, they dig deep into the inner life of the heart to transform us and forge a devotional life that can enable us to fulfill the calling and destiny of our lives.

ENGAGING THE WORLD

Devotional life is not just inward and upward, it is also outward, engaging the world around us. The late Dutch theologian Klaas Runia says that adoration of God "should lead to action in the world, which is another form of worship."[51] As theologian Miroslav Volf summarizes, "Authentic Christian worship takes place in a rhythm of adoration and action."[52] Adoration strengthens our relationship with God because it is two-way communication with him. We come to know God more intimately as we spend time worshipping him. Action brings us into the experience of God in his created world. As we worship God by speaking of his good news with others, creating beauty through art or other disciplines, and serving others, we become the extensions of God's love and goodness into the world and so experience him on a deeper level.

That mission and worship are bound together helps us in another way. All too often we focus so strongly on mission that we become enthralled with it. Our zeal for the work can blind us to our true spiritual condition and make us unaware of how our actions are affecting others. Our missional and devotional lives are connected; each strengthens the other and expresses the other. Devotional life extends the reach of God's kingdom into the world around it, and missional life results in people with a deep and attractive relationship with God. The weight of success and the pain of failure in mission will place the greatest pressure on the weakest areas of character. These are usually the areas in which leaders and followers fall.

When the inner life is weak, it cannot sustain the pressures of failure or success in the outer life for long. Likewise, lack of engagement in mission produces a shallow, irrelevant, and deluded devotional life. Until our ideas about God and life are tested by reality, they are only theoretical. When worship is isolated from mission, we can develop warped ideas about God, life, and people. When we engage in the world, our understanding of reality is tested and reshaped by actual experience. Then our worship is not just in Spirit, but also in truth. If we're not engaged in mission, we're not fully worshipping God.

 To be authentic and complete, devotional life cannot be contained within our private lives or our life in Christian community. It must spill into an outer life that engages the broader world without Christ.

APPENDIX

Table 1

AREAS OF CONTINUITY BETWEEN THE TWO PRIESTHOODS

Continuity between the two priesthoods gives people a common base of comparison to understand the new covenant, as seen in the book of Hebrews.

Point of Comparison	Aaron (Old Covenant)	Jesus Christ (New Covenant)
1. Qualifications of the High Priest		
Solidarity of the priest with people	The priests were taken from men, 5:1	Jesus shared in flesh and blood, 2:14-18
Ability to sympathize with human weakness	5:1-2	Jesus was tempted in every way we are yet did not sin, 4:14-15
Appointed High Priest by God	5:1	5:4-6; 7:28
2. Ministry of the High Priest		
Have something to offer	5:1; 8:3	9:26,28; 10:5
Blood sacrifice offered in the tabernacle	9:11-14	9:24-26
Represented the people to God (including as an intercessor)	5:1	2:17 (7:25; 9:24)

3. Results of the High Priestly Ministry		
Blood sacrifice inaugurates the covenant	9:15-22	9:11-14
Blood brings cleansing in both priesthoods	9:9,13,22	9:14; 10:14

Table 2

AREAS OF DISCONTINUITY BETWEEN THE TWO PRIESTHOODS

Discontinuity between the two priesthoods shows the ways in which the high priesthood of Jesus is superior to that of the old covenant under Aaron, as seen in the book of Hebrews.

Point of Comparison	Aaron (Old Covenant)	Jesus Christ (New Covenant)
1. Qualifications of the High Priest		
Ability to sympathize with human weakness	The high priest is able to only μετριοπαθέω (met·ree·op·ath·eh·o), 5:2	Jesus is able to συμπαθέω (soom·path·eh·o), 4:15
Sinfulness	High priest was sinful, 5:3; 7:27; 9:7	Christ was sinless, 4:15; 7:26-27
Appointed high priest by God	Appointed high priest, 5:1	Appointed Son, 5:5
Method of appointment	Appointed by Law, without an oath, 7:20,28	Appointed by oath, 7:21,22,28
Appointed because of lineage	Descendant of Aaron, 7:11,16	After the order of Melchizedek, 5:6,10; 7:11-17
Permanence	Limited by death, 7:23-24	Lives forever, 7:23-24
Perfection	Weak, 7:28	Perfect, 7:28

2. Ministry of the High Priest		
Sacrifice for sins	Once every year, 9:7,12-13,24-25; 10:1-4	Once for all, 7:27; 9:12; 10:10 (ἐφάπαξ, ef·ap·ax); 9:26,28 (ἅπαξ, ap·ax); also at the end of age, 9:26
What was offered	Animal sacrifices, 9:12-14,25; 10:4	Jesus offered himself as the sacrifice, 7:27; 9:14,25; 10:5-10
3. Results of the High Priestly Ministry		
Blood as the medium of cleansing	Could not perfect the worshipper, especially in the conscience, 7:11,19; 9:9,13-14	Cleansed even to the conscience, 7:11; 9:9,13-14; 10:10,14
Result of the blood sacrifice	Covered the sin, 10:1-4	Took away sin, 10:1-4

BIBLIOGRAPHY

Aland, Kurt, Matthew Black, Carlo Martini, Bruce Metzger, Allen Wikgren, eds. *Novum Testamentum Graece.* 27th ed. Stuttgart, Germany: Deutsche Bibelgesellschaft, 1993.

Attridge, Harold W. *Hebrews.* Philadelphia: Fortress, 1989.

Aune, David E. *Revelation 6–16.* Word Biblical Commentary, vol. 52B. Nashville: Thomas Nelson, 1998.

Bauer, W., F. W. Danker, F. Arndt, and F. W. Gingrich, eds. *A Greek-English Lexicon of the New Testament and Other Early Christian Literature (BDAG).* 3rd ed. Chicago: University of Chicago Press, 2000. In *Accordance.* Altamonte Springs, FL: OakTree Software, CD-ROM, 1.5.

Beale, G. K. *The Book of Revelation.* New International Greek Testament Commentary. Grand Rapids, MI: Eerdmans, 1999.

Brown, Colin, ed. *New International Dictionary of New Testament Theology.* Vol. 2. Grand Rapids, MI: Zondervan, 1979.

Brown, Francis, S. R. Driver, and Charles A. Briggs, eds. *The Brown-Driver-Briggs Hebrew and English Lexicon (BDB).* Oxford: Clarendon Press, 1906. In *Accordance.* Altamonte Springs, FL: OakTree Software, CD-ROM, 2.0.

Carson, D. A. *The Gospel According to John.* Grand Rapids, MI: Eerdmans, 1990.

Charlesworth, James H., ed. *The Old Testament Pseudepigrapha.* Garden City, NY: Doubleday, 1983.

Craig, Peter C. *Psalm 1–50.* Word Biblical Commentary, vol. 19. Waco, TX: Word, 1983.

Downing, Jim. *Meditation*. Colorado Springs, CO: NavPress, 1976.

Dunn, James D. G. *Romans 9–16*. Word Biblical Commentary, vol. 38B. Waco, TX: Word, 1988.

Ellingworth, Paul. *The Epistle to the Hebrews*. New International Greek Testament Commentary. Grand Rapids, MI: Eerdmans, 1993.

Fee, Gordon. *The First Epistle to the Corinthians*. New International Commentary on the New Testament. Grand Rapids, MI: Eerdmans, 1987.

Fujimura, Makoto. *Refractions*. Colorado Springs, CO: NavPress, 2009.

Hattori, Yoshiaki. "Theology of Worship in the Old Testament." In *Worship: Adoration and Action*, edited by D. A. Carson. Grand Rapids, MI: Baker, 2002.

Hill, Andrew E. *Enter His Courts with Praise*. Grand Rapids, MI: Baker, 1993.

Hughes, Graham. *Hebrews and Hermeneutics*. Cambridge, UK: Cambridge University Press, 1979.

Hurst, Lincoln D. *The Epistle to the Hebrews: Its Background of Thought*. Cambridge, UK: Cambridge University Press, 1990.

Keil, C. F., and Franz Delitzsch. *Isaiah*. Commentary on the Old Testament. Vol. 7, no. 2. Grand Rapids, MI: Eerdmans, 1982.

Keil, C. F., and Franz Delitzsch. *Jeremiah, Lamentations*. Commentary on the Old Testament. Vol. 8, no. 2. Grand Rapids, MI: Eerdmans, 1982.

Keil, C. F., and Franz Delitzsch. *The Minor Prophets*. Commentary on the Old Testament. Vol. 10, no. 1. Grand Rapids, MI: Eerdmans, 1982.

Keil, C. F., and Franz Delitzsch. *Proverbs, Ecclesiastes, Song of Solomon*. Commentary on the Old Testament. Vol. 6, no. 3. Grand Rapids, MI: Eerdmans, 1982.

Koester, Craig R. *The Dwelling of God: The Tabernacle in the Old Testament, Intertestamental Jewish Literature, and the New Testament*. Catholic Biblical Quarterly Monograph Series 22. Washington, DC: Catholic Biblical Association, 1989.

Lane, William. *Hebrews 1–8*. Word Biblical Commentary, vol. 47A. Dallas: Word, 1991.

Lane, William. *Hebrews 9–13*. Word Biblical Commentary, vol. 47B. Dallas: Word, 1991.

Lehne, Susanne. "The New Covenant in Hebrews." *Journal for the Study of the New Testament Supplement Series* 44. Sheffield, UK: JSOT Press, 1990.

Lincoln, Andrew T. *Ephesians*. Word Biblical Commentary, vol. 42. Dallas: Word, 1990.

Malone, Fred A. "A Critical Evaluation of the Use of Jeremiah 31:31-34 in the Letter to the Hebrews." PhD diss., Southwestern Baptist Theological Seminary, 1989.

Manley, G. T. "Names of God." In *The New Bible Dictionary*, edited by J. D. Douglas. Grand Rapids, MI: Eerdmans, 1962.

McKnight, Scot. "Justice and Righteousness." In *Dictionary of Jesus and the Gospels*, edited by Joel Green and Scot McKnight. Downers Grove, IL: InterVarsity, 1992.

Metzger, Bruce M. *A Textual Commentary on the Greek New Testament*. Stuttgart, Germany: Biblia Druck, 1971.

Moo, Douglas J. *James*. Tyndale New Testament Commentaries. Grand Rapids, MI: Eerdmans, 1985.

Motyer, J. A. "Names." In *New Bible Dictionary*, 3rd ed., edited by I. Howard Marshall, A. R. Millard, J. I. Packer, and Donald J. Wiseman. University and Colleges Christian Fellowship, 1996. Electronic text hypertexted and prepared by *Accordance*. Altamonte Springs, FL: OakTree Software. Ver. 1.0.

O'Brien, Peter T. *The Epistle to the Philippians*. New International Greek Testament Commentary. Grand Rapids, MI: Eerdmans, 1991.

Peterson, David. "Worship in the New Testament." In *Worship: Adoration and Action*, edited by D. A. Carson. Grand Rapids, MI: Baker, 2002.

Pratt, Dwight M. "Light." In *The International Standard Bible Encyclopedia*, vol. 3, edited by James Orr. Grand Rapids, MI: Eerdmans, 1983.

Runia, Klaas. "The Reformed Dutch Liturgy in the Dutch Tradition." In *Worship: Adoration and Action*, edited by D. A. Carson. Grand Rapids, MI: Baker, 2002.

Scholer, John. "Proleptic Priests." *Journal for the Study of the New Testament Supplement Series* 49, edited by David Hill. Sheffield, UK: JSOT Press, 1991.

Soskice, Janet. *Metaphor and Religious Language*. Oxford, UK: Clarendon Press, 1985.

Strong, James. *The Tabernacle of Israel: Its Structure and Symbolism*. Grand Rapids, MI: Kregel, 1987.

Tate, Marvin E. *Psalms 51–100*. Word Biblical Commentary, vol. 20. Dallas: Word, 1990.

Thompson, J. A. *Book of Jeremiah*. New International Commentary on the Old Testament. Grand Rapids, MI: Eerdmans, 1980.

VanGemeren, Willem A., ed. *New International Dictionary of Old Testament Theology and Exegesis*. Grand Rapids, MI: Zondervan, 1997. Electronic text hypertexted and prepared by *Accordance*. Altamonte Springs, FL: OakTree Software. Ver. 1.0

Volf, Miroslav. "Reflections." In *Worship: Adoration and Action*, edited by D. A. Carson. Grand Rapids, MI: Baker, 2002.

Vos, Geerhardus. "Hebrews, the Epistle of the Diatheke." In *Princeton Theological Review* 14, no. 1. Princeton, NJ: 1916.

Webster's Third New International Dictionary, Unabridged. Springfield, MA: Merriam-Webster, 2000.

Young, Edward J. *The Book of Isaiah*. Vol. 3. Grand Rapids, MI: Eerdmans, 1972.

Young, N. H. "'Tout Estin Sarkos Autou' (Heb.X.20): Apposition, Dependent or Explicative?" In *New Testament Studies*, vol. 20, edited by John Barclay. Cambridge, UK: Cambridge University Press, 1974.

NOTES

CHAPTER 1: THE HOODED CROWS OF RED SQUARE

1. This movement, called the CoMission, recruited more than fourteen hundred people from their everyday lives as teachers, state troopers, grandmothers, and great-grandfathers to join a team of nine others and move to Russia, Ukraine, Latvia, Estonia, Bulgaria, or Kazakhstan to live for one year. At the invitation of the Russian Ministry of Education, we worked with Russian educators to train them to teach a curriculum of ethics and morality that used Jesus as a model citizen and the Bible as a textbook for ethics and morality.

2. *Webster's Third New International Dictionary, Unabridged,* s.v. "disorient," accessed May 26, 2010, http://unabridged.merriam-webster.com.

3. See Psalm 3; 18; 34; 51; 52; 54; 56; 57; 59; 60; 62; 63; 142. You can feel David's dependence on God and his confidence in God growing in these psalms.

4. Luke 4:14; see also Mark 1:9-12; Luke 4:1-13.

5. The word *desert* in the Old Testament is usually translated from the Hebrew word מִדְבָּר (mid·bawr), which means "an uninhabited land." See Francis Brown, S. R. Driver, and Charles A. Briggs, eds., *The Brown-Driver-Briggs Hebrew and English Lexicon (BDB)* (Oxford: Clarendon Press, 1906), in *Accordance* (Altamonte Springs, FL: OakTree Software), CD-ROM, 2.0, s.v. "מִדְבָּר." The Greek Scriptures (Old and New Testaments) use the terms ἐρημία (er·ay·mee·ah) and ἔρημος (er·ay·mos). *Er·ay·mee·ah* means "uninhabited or lonely region, normally with sparse vegetation, desert"; see W. Bauer, F. W. Danker, F. Arndt, and F. W. Gingrich, eds., *A Greek-English Lexicon of the New Testament and Other Early Christian Literature (BDAG),* 3rd ed. (Chicago: University of Chicago Press, 2000), in *Accordance* (Altamonte Springs, FL: OakTree Software), CD-ROM, 1.5, s.v. "ἔρημος." The term ἔρημος (er·ay·mos)

as an adjective means something or someone who is "in a state of isolation, isolated, desolate, deserted." Its feminine noun form means "an uninhabited region or locality, desert, grassland, wilderness"; see *BDAG*, s.v. "ἔρημος."

6. See also Exodus 13:18,21; 15:22; Numbers 10:12; Psalm 78:52; Amos 2:10; Acts 7:36.

7. 2 Samuel 22:31; Psalm 18:30.

8. Exodus 3:12,18; 5:1,3; 7:16; 8:27-28; 12:31.

9. Numbers 1:3,22,24,26,28,30,32,34,36,38,40,42,45; 10:9,13-14; 26:2; 31:3-6,21,27-28,32,36,49,53; 32:6,20,27; Deuteronomy 1:41; 2:14,16; 3:18; 4:34; 20:12,19-20; 21:10-14; 24:5; 31:1-10.

10. A crucible is "a vessel or melting pot of some very refractory material (as clay, graphite, porcelain . . . that is used for melting . . . a substance (as metal and ore) which requires a high degree of heat. . . . Something that tests as if by fire: a severe test or trial," *Webster's Third New International Dictionary, Unabridged*, s.v. "crucible," accessed May 12, 2010, http://unabridged.merriam-webster.com.

11. Isaiah 29:16; Jeremiah 18:1-6; Romans 9:21.

CHAPTER 2: A TRAILER IN A RED CLAY LOT

1. *Man*: "(with reference to the manna) most probably 'What is it?' the question being intended as a popular etymology of מָן הוּא (What is it) to מָן (mawn) 'manna'"; see Francis Brown, S. R. Driver, and Charles A. Briggs, eds., *The Brown-Driver-Briggs Hebrew and English Lexicon (BDB)* (Oxford: Clarendon Press, 1906), in *Accordance* (Altamonte Springs, FL: OakTree Software), CD-ROM, 2.0, s.v. "מָן."

2. In the Hebrew Old Testament the word here for *test* is נָסָה (naw·saw). It means to "test, try, prove, tempt"; see *BDB*. In the Greek text *test* is translated by πειρασμός (pi·ras·mos), meaning "to subject to test or proof, tempt"; see W. Bauer, F. W. Danker, F. Arndt, and F. W. Gingrich, eds., *A Greek-English Lexicon of the New Testament and Other Early Christian Literature (BDAG)*, 3rd ed. (Chicago: University of Chicago Press, 2000), in *Accordance* (Altamonte Springs, FL: OakTree Software), CD-ROM, 1.5. The English word *test* means: "to examine or analyze (a substance) . . . to determine the attributes or performance characteristics of <enough samples must be tested to show how the product performs> Mech. Engineering . . . to examine for disease or physical defect <test a tumor> <test the reflexes>." *Webster's Third New*

International Dictionary, Unabridged, s.v. "test," accessed May 10, 2010, http://unabridged.merriam-webster.com.

3. Deuteronomy 5:29; 6:5-6; 10:12-16; 30:6. This theme of the importance of the heart can be seen throughout the Scriptures; see 1 Samuel 16:7; 1 Kings 8:61; Psalm 78:37; Jeremiah 24:7; 31:33-34; Ezekiel 36:26-27; Matthew 22:37-38; Mark 12:30,33; Luke 10:27; Acts 13:22; Ephesians 3:16-17.

4. Proverbs 4:23. The word here, תּוֹצָאוֹת (to·tsaw·aw), means "sources of life," *BDB.*

5. The word here, ἀπιστία (ap·is·tee·ah), means "unwillingness to commit oneself to another or respond positively to the other's words or actions, lack of belief, unbelief"; see *BDAG,* s.v. "ἀπιστία."

6. Exodus 17:6-7.

7. Job 5:17.

8. Proverbs 12:1.

9. Hebrews 12:11.

10. Numbers 11:33. Israel even named this location Kibroth Hattavah, meaning "graves of desire" or "graves of craving."

11. Numbers 11:23.

CHAPTER 3: TREASURE IN THE DESERT

1. The English word "refuge" or "stronghold" is rendered from the Hebrew word מִשְׂגָּב (mis·gawb), meaning "secure height, retreat . . . a stronghold. . . . Fig of God as refuge" in these verses: Psalm 9:9; 18:2 (cf. 2 Samuel 22:3); Psalm 46:7,11; 48:3; 59:9,16-17; 62:2,7; 94:22; 144:2. See Francis Brown, S. R. Driver, and Charles A. Briggs, eds., *The Brown-Driver-Briggs Hebrew and English Lexicon (BDB)* (Oxford: Clarendon Press, 1906), in *Accordance* (Altamonte Springs, FL: OakTree Software), CD-ROM, 2.0, s.v. "מִשְׂגָּב."

2. *Webster's Third New International Dictionary, Unabridged,* s.v. "sanctuary," accessed April 28, 2010, http://unabridged.merriam-webster.com.

3. Pavilion: Psalm 18:11 (KJV, pavilion; NIV, canopy); 27:5 (KJV, pavilion; NIV, dwelling); 31:20 (KJV, pavilion; NIV, dwelling); Shelter: Psalm 31:20 (NIV); 61:3 (KJV); 61:4; 91:1, "He who dwells in the shelter of the Most High will rest in the shadow of the Almighty" (NIV); Hiding Place: Psalm 32:7; 119:114 (KJV); Secret Place: Psalm 18:11 (KJV); 27:5 (KJV, "secret of his tabernacle"); 91:1(KJV); Secret of His Presence: Psalm 31:20 (KJV); Shadow: Psalm 91:1; Isaiah 51:16; Wings: Ruth 2:12; Psalm 17:8; 36:7;

57:1; 61:4; 63:7; 91:4; Stronghold: 1 Samuel 22:5; 24:22; 2 Samuel
5:17; 22:3; 23:14; 1 Chronicles 11:16; 12:8,16; Job 39:28;
Psalm 9:9; 18:2; 27:1; 37:39; 43:2; 52:7; 144:2; Ezekiel 24:21; Strong
Tower: Psalm 61:3; Proverbs 18:10.

4. Our English word *sanctuary* is translated from two words in the Hebrew
text of the Old Testament: מִקְדָּשׁ (mik·dawsh) and קֹדֶשׁ (ko·desh).
מִקְדָּשׁ (mik·dawsh) means "a sacred place, sanctuary," see *BDB*, s.v.
"מִקְדָּשׁ." קֹדֶשׁ (ko·desh) means "apartness, sacredness, holiness of
God . . . of places set apart as sacred by God's presence," see *BDB*, s.v.
"קֹדֶשׁ." *Sanctuary* is translated from two words in the Greek Old
Testament (the Septuagint): ἁγίασμα (hag·ee·as·mos) means "a space set
aside for devotion, sanctuary"; see W. Bauer, F. W. Danker, F. Arndt,
and F. W. Gingrich, eds., *A Greek-English Lexicon of the New Testament
and Other Early Christian Literature (BDAG)*, 3rd ed. (Chicago:
University of Chicago Press, 2000), in *Accordance* (Altamonte Springs,
FL: OakTree Software), CD-ROM, 1.5, s.v. "ἁγίασμα." The word
ἅγιος (hag·ee·os) means "being dedicated or consecrated to the service
of God . . . holy."

5. The Hebrew word for *holy* is קֹדֶשׁ (ko·desh), and the words for *sanctuary*
are קֹדֶשׁ (ko·desh) and מִקְדָּשׁ (mik·dawsh), both forms of the word קֹדֶשׁ
(ko·desh). The Greek term for *holy* is ἅγιος (hag·ee·os), and the words
for sanctuary are *hagiasma* and *hagios*. So in both languages the words for
sanctuary are forms of the word *holy*, קֹדֶשׁ (ko·desh) and ἅγιος
(hag·ee·os).

6. קָדַשׁ (kaw·dash) means "separate from human infirmity, impurity," *BDB*,
s.v. "קָדַשׁ."

7. See also Exodus 15:17; 2 Chronicles 36:15; Habbakuk 2:20.

8. See 1 Kings 8:17,29,43; 1 Chronicles 22:19; 2 Chronicles 20:8-9;
Psalm 74:7.

9. "The name is no mere label, but is significant of the real personality of
him to whom it belongs. It may derive from the circumstances of his
birth (Gn. 5:29), or reflect his character (Gn. 27:36), and when a person
puts his 'name' upon a thing or another person the latter comes under
his influence and protection," G. T. Manley, "Names of God," in *The
New Bible Dictionary*, ed. J. D. Douglas (Grand Rapids, MI: Eerdmans,
1962), 478.

10. See Genesis 17:5; 18:18; Galatians 3:8.

11. See, for example, Exodus 6:2-3 (Yahweh); 17:10-15 (Jehovah-Nissi).

12. "In form the divine name Yahweh is either a simple indicative or a causative indicative of the verb 'to be,' meaning 'he is (alive, present, active)' or 'he brings into being,' and the formula in which the name is disclosed (Exodus 3:14, I AM WHO I AM) means either 'I reveal my active presence as and when I will' or 'I bring to pass what I choose to bring to pass,'" J. A. Motyer, "Names," in *The New Bible Dictionary*, ed. I. Howard Marshall, A. R. Millard, J. I. Packer, and Donald J. Wiseman, 3rd ed. (University and Colleges Christian Fellowship, 1996, electronic text hypertexted and prepared by OakTree Software [Altamonte Springs, FL], CD-ROM, 1.0). See also Exodus 6:2-3 where God gives fuller and more personal depth to the name that the patriarchs had not known as he was now revealing to Moses.

13. See also Psalm 99:5; 132:7-9; Isaiah 60:13; 66:1; Lamentations 2:1.

14. Psalm 63:2. See also Psalm 29:9; Revelation 15:8.

15. 1 Kings 8:10-13.

16. See Exodus 29:43; 40:34-35; Leviticus 9:23; Numbers 14:10; 16:19,42; 20:6.

17. See Psalm 5:7; 48:9; 134:2; 150:1.

18. See Exodus 25:1–31:18. *Sanctuary* can refer to the tabernacle and its courts (with the Hebrew word קֹדֶשׁ [ko·desh] in Exodus 40:9; Numbers 3:28; or with the word מִשְׁכָּן [mish·kawn] in Exodus 25:8; Leviticus 16:33; 21:23). It can refer to the tabernacle alone (Exodus 38:24; Leviticus 10:4); the courtyard (Leviticus 10:17-18); the outer room of the tabernacle (the Holy Place) (Exodus 26:33; 28:29); and it can refer to the inner room of the tabernacle (the Holiest of All) (Leviticus 4:6; 16:2,33).

19. See Exodus 24:1-18; 25:1–31:18.

20. *Sanctuary* can refer to the temple by itself (2 Chronicles 29:5; Isaiah 64:11; 1 Chronicles 29:3; Psalm 5:7; see also Psalm 138:2; 79:1), or it can include the courts surrounding the temple (2 Chronicles 29:7; Daniel 8:13; Isaiah 43:28; 1 Chronicles 24:5; Psalm 60:8, which is identical to 108:8). In the following verses the phrase קֹדֶשׁ (ko·desh) מִשְׁכָּן (mish·kawn) is translated "temple": 1 Chronicles 22:19; Isaiah 63:18; Psalm 74:7. It can also refer to the outer room of the temple (1 Kings 8:10; see also 2 Chronicles 5:11), the inner room (Ezekiel 41:4,21,23; Psalm 28:2; 1 Kings 6:16; 7:50; 8:6; 2 Chronicles 3:8,10; 4:22; 5:7), or the temple's court of the priests (Ezekiel 42:14; 44:27; Isaiah 62:9).

21. See also 2 Chronicles 6:21,30,33,39; 30:27.

22. The Hebrew preposition in this verse is בְּ (bĕ). I prefer the meaning "into" here, not "to." This is not only because the primary sense of בְּ (bĕ) is "in," but also because of the imagery of the context. A strong tower would do someone no good if he simply ran up to it and stopped. The value of a strong tower is that it is a place that you can enter and be protected from threats. The imagery of this verse makes better sense with the meaning "into." See *BDB*, s.v. "בְּ."

23. We've already seen verses that refer to God's dwelling in heaven as a "sanctuary" (e.g., Psalm 102:19; cf. 1 Kings 8:30,39,43). God was giving a spatial model on earth of what was in heaven and God himself was the nexus between the heavenly and earthly sanctuaries, because it was he that dwelt in them both. We will discuss this in chapter 4.

24. Jim Downing, *Meditation* (Colorado Springs, CO: NavPress, 1976), 56–60.

25. Exodus 33:20; Judges 13:22.

CHAPTER 4: PASSPORT TO AN UNSHAKABLE KINGDOM

1. Franz Delitzsch writes, "[God] has also established in man an impulse leading him beyond that which is temporal toward the eternal: it lies in his nature not to be contented with the temporal, but to break through the limits which it draws around him, to escape from the bondage and the disquietude within which he is held . . . by directing his thoughts to eternity," *Proverbs, Ecclesiastes, Song of Solomon*, Commentary on the Old Testament, vol. 6, no. 3 (Grand Rapids, MI: Eerdmans, 1982), 261.

2. We find sanctuary imagery throughout the Psalms in the words of David describing the worship of God with the language of the offerings, altars, incense, priests, and the courts of the tabernacle. The prophets pick up this imagery from Isaiah's vision of the exalted Lord in his temple (Isaiah 6:1-8) to the elaborate visions of Ezekiel and the glory of God departing and returning to the temple (Ezekiel 10; 40–43). The following examples give us a taste of the sanctuary imagery in the Minor Prophets. The sanctuary: Daniel 8:11,13-14; 9:17,26; 11:31; Zephaniah 3:4; the temple: Daniel 5:2-3; Amos 8:3; Jonah 2:4,7; Micah 1:2; Habbakuk 2:20; Haggai 2:15,18; Zechariah 6:12-15; 8:9; Malachi 3:1; priests: Joel 1:13; 2:17, and twenty-eight more occurrences; the altar: Joel 1:13; 2:17; Amos 2:8; 3:14; 9:1; Zechariah 9:15; 14:20; Malachi 1:7,10; 2:13; and the lampstand: Zechariah 4:2.

3. Revelation 19:11-13 refers to Jesus in his glorified state. He is described as wearing clothing characteristic of the high priest. See Geerhardus Vos, "Hebrews, the Epistle of the Diatheke," *Princeton Theological Review* 14, no. 1 (1916): 20.

4. Hebrews 12:24; see also 8:6; 9:15.

5. Outside of the book of Hebrews the sanctuary imagery appears in the writings of the apostle John, in several of Paul's letters, and in the book of Acts. In John's gospel when the Son of God dwells among men, the term used is σκηνόω (skay·no·o). This word comes from the root of the word *tabernacle* (σκήνωμα [skay·no·mah]) and the related term σκηνή (skay·nay), which is also usually translated as *tent*. It is interesting to note, in this respect, that *skay·no·mah* is used in 2 Peter 1:13-14 for the human body, which parallels John's usage here. In John 2:13-22, Christ's cleansing of the temple carries a typological sense; Jesus is fulfilling the purpose of the temple and replacing it (see D. A. Carson, *The Gospel According to John* [Grand Rapids, MI: Eerdmans, 1990], 182). In Revelation, John describes the redeemed as those who dwell (the same verb as in John 1:14) in the heavens where God tabernacles (again *skay·no·o*) over them (7:25). See Craig R. Koester, *The Dwelling of God: The Tabernacle in the Old Testament, Intertestamental Jewish Literature, and the New Testament*, Catholic Biblical Quarterly Monograph Series 22 (Washington, DC: Catholic Biblical Association, 1989), 115, 120–123, 131. The Apocalypse also contains the concept of the tabernacle-city (21:1-9).

Paul uses the model of the temple (ναός [nah·os]) to describe both the Christian community (1 Corinthians 3:16-17; Ephesians 2:21; 2 Corinthians 6:16) and the body of the individual Christian (1 Corinthians 6:19) as places God dwells by his Spirit.

In the book of Acts, Luke mentions the "tent [skay·nay] of David" that is fallen, applying Amos 9:11-12 to the Jew-Gentile struggle in the regions of southern Galatia and Antioch. In Acts 7 we find a use of sanctuary imagery that is closer to that of the book of Hebrews. Stephen denounces temple worship in his day because it attempts to confine God to the temple of Israel (Acts 7:44-50). So, both Acts and Hebrews address the same problem: "treating as final and ultimate what God intended to be earthly and provisional." See Lincoln D. Hurst, *The Epistle to the Hebrews: Its Background of Thought* (Cambridge: Cambridge University Press, 1990), 97.

6. Vos, *Princeton Theological Review* 13, no. 4 (1915): 587–632; and 14, no. 1 (1916): 1–61.

7. See Susanne Lehne, "The New Covenant in Hebrews," *Journal for the Study of the New Testament Supplement Series* 44 (Sheffield, UK: JSOT Press, 1990), 87.

8. We find allusions to the new covenant in Matthew 26:28; Mark 14:24; Luke 22:20; 1 Corinthians 11:25; Romans 11:27; 2 Corinthians 3:6; Galatians 4:24. The word for covenant (dee·ath·ay·kay) also occurs in Luke 1:72; Acts 3:25; 7:8; Romans 9:4; 2 Corinthians 3:14; Galatians 3:15,17; Ephesians 2:12; Revelation 11:19. In these verses, though, it refers only to aspects of the old covenant, or other covenants in the Old Testament.

9. *Webster's Third New International Dictionary, Unabridged,* s.v. "covenant," accessed June 12, 2010, http://unabridged.merriam-webster.com.

10. In Hebrews 7 we are told that the old covenant system was weak and could not make the worshipper perfect, despite its sacrifices (7:11,18-19). In chapter 8 the new covenant quotation is introduced by saying that something was wrong with the first covenant, and that it would be replaced. Hebrews 9 tells us that the sacrifices of the old covenant could not cleanse the worshipper's conscience, and that these sacrifices were temporary until the perfect sacrifice appeared in Christ. The way into heaven had to be "cleansed" with better sacrifices than the old covenant could provide (Hebrews 9:9-10,23-24). The Law was only a shadow of the good things to come and could not perfect the worshippers (Hebrews 10:1).

11. Hebrews 10:1,4,9-12,14,18.

12. This book will not tackle a full exegesis of the new covenant in Jeremiah or in the epistle of Hebrews. For a closer look at these themes see Lehne, 19–124, and Fred A. Malone, "A Critical Evaluation of the Use of Jeremiah 31:31-34 in the Letter to the Hebrews" (PhD diss., Southwestern Baptist Theological Seminary, 1989).

13. While the recipients of the new covenant prophecy in Jeremiah were Judah and Israel (see Jeremiah 31:31), it is clear that a much broader reference is intended by the quotation in the book of Hebrews. As Malone observes, "To restrict these broader terms only to Jews places the interpreter in the untenable position that the new covenant blessings in Hebrews are for Jewish Christians and future Jews but not for gentile Christians"; see Malone, 180. An expanded meaning of Israel and Judah

is also suggested by the use of first-person plural pronouns ἡμῖν (hay·meen) (Hebrews 10:15) and ἔχοντες ... ἡμῖν (ech·o·ntes) (Hebrews 10:19-20) to refer to recipients of the new covenant, and the change from Israel and Judah (Hebrews 8:8) to αὐτούς (ow·tos) (Hebrews 10:16); see Malone, 179–180. Further, he argues that the typological comparisons of Israel and Judah to Christian believers (Hebrews 3:7–4:11; 10:28-29; 11:1–12:2,25) are sufficient "to justify application of Jeremiah 31:31-34 to Christians along the imperfect-perfect, old covenant-new covenant, type-antitype continuum," Malone, 181.

14. Exodus 24:12; 31:18; 32:15-16,19; 34:1,4,28-29; Deuteronomy 4:13; 5:22; 9:9-11,15,17; 10:1-5.

15. Deuteronomy 5:29; 6:5-6; 10:12-16; Isaiah 29:13; Joel 2:13.

16. Romans 3:19-20; Galatians 3:21-22.

17. C. F. Keil, *Jeremiah, Lamentations*, Commentary on the Old Testament, vol. 8, no. 2 (Grand Rapids, MI: Eerdmans, 1982), 38.

18. Jeremiah 32:39; 31:31-34; Ezekiel 11:19; 36:26; 2 Corinthians 5:17.

19. In Hebrews 2:9-17 Jesus, as the merciful and faithful High Priest, tastes death for everyone to bring sons and daughters into his family, making them holy. Therefore he is not ashamed to call them his brothers.

20. See for example, the prophets: Moses, Deuteronomy 34:10; and Samuel, 1 Samuel 3:21–4:1; 7:5; 8:6-22; 16:1-13; King David, 2 Samuel 23:2; the priests: Exodus 28:29-30; 1 Samuel 28:6; Ezra 2:63; Nehemiah 7:65 (the high priest, with Urim and Thummim, would seek the will of God for the people at times; the priests also taught the Law, as did Ezra [7:1-10]).

21. The Hebrew verb used here, יָדַע (yaw·day), has an experiential sense. It means to "know, learn to know"; see Francis Brown, S. R. Driver, and Charles A. Briggs, eds., *The Brown-Driver-Briggs Hebrew and English Lexicon (BDB)* (Oxford: Clarendon Press, 1906), in *Accordance* (Altamonte Springs, FL: OakTree Software), CD-ROM, 2.0, s.v. "יָדַע." It also has a sense of moral responsibility as in Jeremiah 22:15-16.

22. Exodus 6:7; 10:2; 16:6.

23. See William Lane, *Hebrews 9–13*, Word Biblical Commentary, vol. 47B (Dallas: Word, 1991), 488–491.

24. Janet Soskice explains that a model uses an object or state of affairs as a way of viewing some other object or state of affairs; see Janet Soskice, *Metaphor and Religious Language* (Oxford, UK: Clarendon Press, 1985), 55. A model

makes complex concepts intelligible and enables a writer to describe what is unobservable or transcendent. We create metaphorical language when we speak or write using the reality represented by a model; see Soskice, 54–55, 103–108. So the model of fatherhood is the basis for speaking metaphorically of God as caring, loving, nurturing, and disciplining us as his children.

25. The work of Graham Hughes (*Hebrews and Hermeneutics* [Cambridge, UK: Cambridge University Press, 1979], 8–10, 26, 46–47, 66) is helpful on this point. He proposes that the author of Hebrews sets up a dialectical relationship of continuity-discontinuity between old and new covenant revelation. The covenants are continuous in that they both represent forms of God's address to his people in one ongoing history of salvation. They are discontinuous in that they are separated by the "eschatological division between the ages" (Hughes, *Hermeneutics*, 66), which came in the perfect form of God's address in Jesus Christ. Angels are compared to Christ as mediators of the law-covenant. Continuity exists in that with both covenants the same word demands a response. Discontinuity exists in that the mediators (angels and Jesus) are accorded different degrees of dignity. Moses and Christ share continuity in that the location of their ministries is the house of God, but are different in that Moses is a "servant in the house," while Christ is a "Son over the house." As is mentioned in note 20 on page 169, the priests both represented the people before God and represented God to the people by using the Urim and Thummin to seek the will of God and declare it to his people.

For further discussion of the comparisons of Jesus and the Aaronic high priesthood, see Hebrews 2:17; 3:1; 4:14-16; 5:1-10; 7:1-28.

We see the third comparison of Jesus as High Priest with the old covenant high priests in the middle chapters of Hebrews. There the author ties the covenant and high priestly themes together very closely before he first mentions the word *covenant* (Hebrews 7:22). He does this by presenting a fascinating comparison of Jesus and the old covenant high priests. There are points of continuity between Jesus and the former high priests. Like the old covenant high priests, Jesus was appointed by God, he offered a blood sacrifice for the sins of the people, and he established a covenant with God's people by a blood sacrifice. See table 1 in the appendix for more detail. There were, though, significant differences between Jesus and his predecessors. Jesus was appointed by God as a Son, and not merely a high priest. Jesus did not offer animals to God as a sacrifice for sin, he offered himself. The blood of the old covenant sacrifices could not take away sins as Jesus' blood did. Table 2 in the appendix provides more detail.

26. We can see this because in all but three of the occurrences of *law* in the epistle it refers to the ministry of the priests or the high priest in the tabernacle area. Of the fourteen occurrences of νόμος (nom·os) in Hebrews all describe the priestly ministry except Hebrews 8:10 and 10:16, which quote the new covenant from Jeremiah, and Hebrews10:28, which is a general reference to Mosaic Law. For further discussion see Lehne, 99.

27. This close relationship of the Law and the priesthood in Hebrews is reciprocal: the Law establishes the priesthood (Hebrews 7:5,12,16,28; 8:4; 9:22), and yet it is the priesthood that carries out the requirements of the Law for dealing with sin and relating to God (Hebrews 7:11-12). So the Law is spoken of primarily in terms of the ministry of the priests in the sanctuary area, and the context of the giving of the Law and the establishment of the priesthood was the scene at Mount Sinai where God made a covenant with his people by sacrifice. See Exodus 24 and Psalm 50:5.

28. This discussion begins in Hebrews 7:1-28.

29. Hebrews 8:5. Here we see again the theme of continuity-discontinuity. The tabernacle of the old covenant is on earth while the tabernacle of Jesus is in heaven (discontinuity), different locations. But we see that the two tabernacles are the dwelling place of God (continuity), the same God present in both.

30. The theme of Christ as mediator is one that is picked up two other times in Hebrews (9:15; 12:24).

31. Hebrews 9 uses the model of the tabernacle to explain the effect of this new level of cleansing: "But only the high priest entered the inner room, and that only once a year, and never without blood, which he offered for himself and for the sins the people had committed in ignorance" (verse 7); "The Holy Spirit was showing by this that the way into the Most Holy Place had not yet been disclosed as long as the first tabernacle was still standing" (verse 8); and "This is an illustration for the present time, indicating that the gifts and sacrifices being offered were not able to clear the conscience of the worshiper" (verse 9).

Here, the author of Hebrews uses the internal layout of the

tabernacle as a model to explain a different level of access to God for those in the new covenant. In Hebrews 9:9 the word *illustration* (NIV) is παραβολή (par·ab·ol·ay), meaning "something that serves as a model or example pointing beyond itself for later realization, *type, figure*"; see W. Bauer, F. W. Danker, F. Arndt, and F. W. Gingrich, eds., *A Greek-English Lexicon of the New Testament and Other Early Christian Literature (BDAG)*, 3rd ed. (Chicago: University of Chicago Press, 2000), in *Accordance* (Altamonte Springs, FL: OakTree Software), CD-ROM, 1.5, s.v. "παραβολή." The tabernacle was divided into two compartments: the Holy Place and the Holiest of All. He says that entrance into the inner chamber, the Holiest of All, was not open while the old covenant system of worship and sacrifice was in place. He explains the reason—the gifts and sacrifices could not cleanse the conscience of the worshipper, making him or her fit to enter the sacred inner chamber. Hebrews 10:1 further develops this theme explaining that the Law could not perfect those who drew near to God to worship (Hebrews 7:11,18-19,28; 10:1,8) because the sacrifices prescribed by the old covenant could not take away sin; see Hebrews 7:19; 10:2-4. The Hebrew word for atonement, כִּפֻּרִים (kip·poor), means to cover; see Leviticus 16:6,10-11,16,17(*bis*),18,24,27. The noun form of this verb combines with the Hebrew word for *day* to give us the familiar phrase יוֹם הַכִּפֻּרִים (yome kip·poor), the Day of Atonement, which means the day the sins of Israel are covered for a year by the blood of a sacrifice according to God's Word in the Old Covenant. These sacrifices did not cleanse the heart and mind. But when Jesus came into the world he did not use animals for the sacrifice; instead, God provided Jesus with a human body, which he offered as the perfect sacrifice for sin (Hebrews 10:5-10). The blood of Jesus in the new covenant, then, perfects the worshipper by cleansing the conscience from sin, which accomplishes a much deeper and complete change of the inner person.

32. Hebrews 9:9; 10:1,14.
33. The priests were to minister in the Holy Place (Exodus 27:20-21; Leviticus 24:2), but only the high priest could enter the Holiest of All (Leviticus 16:1-2,11-19).
34. Nadab and Abihu were killed, leaving Aaron only two sons, Eleazar and Ithamar (Leviticus 10:1-6). These are not the only accounts of people who approached God's presence in an unauthorized manner. Consider Uzziah, king of Judah, who entered the temple to offer incense, which

the king was not permitted to do. He was struck with leprosy until the day he died (2 Chronicles 26:16-21). Then there was the death of Uzzah in 2 Samuel 6:1-7 who was struck down when he touched the ark of the covenant when the cart carrying it shook.

35. Matthew 27:51; Mark 15:38; Luke 23:45.

36. Remember that the author of Hebrews sandwiches an explanation of the superiority of Christ's high priestly ministry (9:1–10:18) between two quotations of Jeremiah's new covenant prophecy (8:8-12 and 10:15-17). This rhetorical device, known as an *inclusio*, shows the author's intent to connect the new covenant prophecy with the explanation of Jesus' high priestly ministry contained between the quotes. This sets up the author to introduce the privileges of the new covenant relationship in terms of the sanctuary imagery (Hebrews 10:19-25).

37. The phrase "great priest" is a common way of referring to the high priest in the Septuagint; see 2 Kings 12:10 where it refers to Jehoiada, the high priest. It is also used for Hilkiah the high priest (2 Kings 22:4,8; 23:4; 2 Chronicles 34:9) and Joshua the high priest in Haggai 1:1,14; 2:2,4; Zechariah 3:1,8; 6:11. In the Pentateuch it appears in Leviticus 21:10 and Numbers 35:25,28,32. See Paul Ellingworth, *The Epistle to the Hebrews,* New International Greek Testament Commentary (Grand Rapids, MI: Eerdmans, 1993), 521–522.

38. Hebrews 1:3,13; 8:1; 10:12; 12:2.

39. In the phrase "through the curtain, that is, his body," the genitive phrase τῆς σαρκὸς αὐτοῦ (tees sark·os ow·too) ([of] his body) is instrumental; it was the death of Jesus that opened the new and living way into the Holiest of All. See Lane, 284, and N. H. Young, "'Tout Estin Sarkos Autou' (Heb.X.20): Apposition, Dependent or Explicative?" *New Testament Studies* 20 (1974), 104.

CHAPTER 5: A MODEL FOR DEVOTIONAL LIFE, PART 1

1. What Paul does here is masterful and sheds significant light on worship in the New Testament. James D. G. Dunn's comments are helpful: "The sacrifice God looks for is no longer that of beast or bird in temple. . . . The boundary of cultic ritual is transposed from actual cultic practices to the life of every day and transformed into nonritual expression, into the much more demanding work of human relationships in an everyday world," James D. G. Dunn, *Romans 9–16*, Word Biblical Commentary, vol. 38B (Waco, TX: Word Press, 1988), 717.

2. We can describe "working out our salvation" to mean applying the sacrifice of Christ in our daily lives to complete the work of transforming us into his image for the glory of God. The apostle Paul here is not saying that we must work to earn our salvation as if we could ever add anything to the death of Jesus to atone for our sins. He is helping us understand that the work of Christ on the cross has an ongoing effect that results in spiritual growth and maturity as we follow and apply his will in our lives. The result of this process is that we grow more and more into the image of Jesus by the work of the Holy Spirit in us. See Romans 8:29; 2 Corinthians 3:18; Galatians 2:20.

3. The twelve tribes camped in this fashion: on the north, Naphtali, Asher, Dan; on the west, Benjamin, Manasseh, Ephraim; on the south, Gad, Simeon, Reuben; and on the east, Zebulun, Issachar, Judah. See Numbers 2:1-34.

4. The middle ring was formed by the Levite families and their camps: On the north the family of Merari camped (Numbers 3:35), then Gershom on the west (Numbers 3:23), followed by the families of Kohath on the south (Numbers 3:29). On the east side Aaron and Moses and their families camped (Numbers 3:36-38). These were the families of the priests and Moses' family. We will explain the priesthood shortly.

5. Merari cared for the frames of the tabernacle, crossbars, posts, bases, all its equipment, everything related to their use, the posts of the courtyard and their bases, the tent pegs and ropes (Numbers 3:33-37). Gershom maintained the tent, coverings, curtains, and their equipment (Numbers 3:25-26). Kohath took care of the sanctuary, the ark of the covenant, the golden table, the golden lampstand, the altars, the articles of the sanctuary used in ministering, the curtain, and everything related to their use (Numbers 3:27-32).

6. Romans 5:12; 7:18-21.

7. Isaiah 6:3; Revelation 4:8.

8. Numbers 1:51; 3:10; 3:38; 18:7.

9. Exodus 28:1; Numbers 3:10; 4:5-15. Carrying the ark of the covenant was a priestly duty; see Deuteronomy 10:8; 31:9; Joshua 3:3,6,8, 13-15,17; 4:9-11,15-18; 1 Kings 2:26; 8:3-7; 1 Chronicles 15:2-3, 12,14-15. Their other duties included:

    (1) Overseeing the worship in the tabernacle/temple including:

        (a) taking care of the oil of the lampstand, the incense, the grain offerings, the anointing oil, and the entire tabernacle, including all its furnishings (Eleazar's duties, Numbers 4:16); (b) keeping the lamp burning through the night (Exodus 27:20-21; Leviticus 24:2-4); (c) ministering at the bronze altar and officiating over the system of sacrifices (Leviticus 4–5; 6:8-12), including the grain and drink offerings (Exodus 29:38-46); (d) eating the showbread in a holy place (Leviticus 24:5-9); (e) burning incense to God at the time the lamp was extinguished in the evenings and lit in the mornings (Exodus 30:1-10); (f) leading Israel in corporate worship during the festivals and feast days and pronouncing blessings on the people (Exodus 40:12-15; Leviticus 1–10; Deuteronomy 10:8; 21:5).

(2) Carrying out the health-related supervision and care of Israel according to the Law (Leviticus 11–15); Numbers 5 (see also Andrew E. Hill, *Enter His Courts with Praise* [Grand Rapids, MI: Baker, 1993], 143, 148).

(3) Serving as mediators between God and the people, representing the people to God (e.g., Yom Kippur, Leviticus 16), and representing God to the people (1 Samuel 8).

(4) Teaching and interpreting the Law (Deuteronomy 17:8-13,18; 27:9-10).

(5) Serving as advisers and counselors to the kings in discerning God's will (Deuteronomy 20:2; Judges 18:18-19; 1 Samuel 14:36-37; 21:6-9; 2 Kings 22 [especially verse 13]; Jeremiah 18:18).

(6) Helping serve in certain legal cases (Deuteronomy 21:5).

10. Leviticus 16:11-19.

11. Leviticus 16:1-9; Hebrews 9:7.

12. Priests were to be the descendants of Aaron (Exodus 28:1-3; Numbers 3:10; 18:7).

13. Exodus 19:5-6.

14. While this is not a point the author of the book of Hebrews makes, it is taught clearly elsewhere in the New Testament: 1 Peter 2:9; Revelation 1:6; 5:10; 20:6.

15. Hebrews 9:9,14; 10:2,22.

16. The courtyard was 100 cubits by 50 cubits in length or 150 feet by 75 feet. I am using a rough cubit measure of 18 inches for ease of calculation. James Strong in *The Tabernacle of Israel: Its Structure and Symbolism* (Grand Rapids, MI: Kregel, 1987), 16, specifies the length of the cubit at 20.63 inches or 1.72 feet based on extant artifacts from the ancient

world, which give a standard for the cubit. In this book I will use, instead, rough estimates based on an 18-inch cubit for simpler estimations.

17. This curtain hung 7.5 feet high and was about 30 feet long (Exodus 38:18-20).

18. Hebrews 10:19-20.

19. John 14:6.

20. Hebrews 10:19-20: "Therefore, brothers, since we have confidence to enter the Most Holy Place by the blood of Jesus, by a new and living way opened for us through the curtain, that is, his body."

21. Psalm 27:4, KJV.

22. Romans 1:25, but it is better to read verses 20-25.

23. Psalm 19:1-6. I would also suggest that man-made beauty also points to the Creator (capital "C") who enables the work of creators (lowercase "c") who are made in his image. Sin has marred that image, yet God's common grace and goodness enable many who are not believers to do marvelous works of art, mathematics, music, and more, though they themselves never appreciate the full beauty of their own work.

24. The Hebrew words here are כָּבוֹד (kaw·bode), "glory," and תִּפְאֶרֶת (tif·aw·raw), "beauty." *Kabod* is the usual word for glory in the Old Testament and is the word used to describe God as a God of glory (e.g., Exodus 16:10; 24:16-17; 29:43; 1 Kings 8:11; Isaiah 6:3). תִּפְאֶרֶת (tif·aw·raw) means beauty or glory as in the beauty or finery of garments and accessories (Isaiah 3:18; 52:1) or jewels (Ezekiel 16:17,39; 23:26, cf. 2 Chronicles 3:6). See Francis Brown, S. R. Driver, and Charles A. Briggs, eds., *The Brown-Driver-Briggs Hebrew and English Lexicon (BDB)* (Oxford: Clarendon Press, 1906), in *Accordance* (Altamonte Springs, FL: OakTree Software), CD-ROM, 2.0, s.v. "תִּפְאֶרֶת."

25. See 1 Chronicles 16:29; 2 Chronicles 20:21; Psalm 29:2; 96:9. The Hebrew phrase repeated in each of these references is בְּהַדְרַת־קֹדֶשׁ (had·aw·raw·at ko·desh) except that in 2 Chronicles 20:21 the preposition בְּ (b-), *in*, is replaced with the preposition לְ (l-), *to*. *Qodesh* of course means "holy," and the word הָדָר (haw·dawr) means "adornment, glory"; see *BDB*, s.v. "הָדָר." As Tate summarizes it can also be taken as "holy attire"; see Marvin E. Tate, *Psalms 51–100*, Word Biblical Commentary, vol. 20 (Dallas: Word, 1990), 511; also C. F. Keil and Franz Delitzsch, *Psalms*, Commentary on the Old Testament, vol. 5

(Grand Rapids, MI: Eerdmans, 1982), 366–368. Tate (511) also rightly points out that the phrase "in his courts" at the end of Psalm 96:8 indicates that in verse 9 the words "worship the Lord in the beauty of holiness" (KJV) or "splendor of his holiness" (NIV) are a reference to the Lord, not the worshipper, as it is sometimes taken. It is interesting that the Septuagint translates this Hebrew phrase into Greek as ἐν αὐλῇ ἁγίᾳ αὐτοῦ (en ow·lay hag·ee·ia ow·too), "in his holy courts." It seems clear that this phrase highlights an aspect of God's holiness, namely that it is beautiful and adorns the person of God like the regal attire of a king. This, then, is the atmosphere of the courts and the holy tabernacle where the Lord dwells.

26. The bronze altar was a square box of acacia wood (7.5 feet by 7.5 feet and 4.5 feet tall). On the four corners of the altar were horns, which we know served to anchor the sacrifices to the altar as they were burned (Psalm 118:27). The altar had a ledge around it 2.25 feet high for the priests to stand on, and a metal grate inside it upon which the sacrifices lay. The altar was also outfitted with rings and poles for transport when the tabernacle moved (Exodus 27:1-8).

27. The word *atone* (Hebrew, כָּפַר [kaw·far]) means to cover. Here it refers to the act of covering a person's sin. We will discuss this in more detail as we continue.

28. In some types of offerings certain parts of the animals were kept to serve as food for the priests. See, for example, the food eaten when Aaron and his sons were consecrated as priests (Exodus 29:31-37; Leviticus 8:31-36). A portion of the grain offering was burned up to the Lord on the altar, but the remaining portion was food for the priests' families (Leviticus 2:1-10). Also, some parts of offerings, like the fellowship offering, were for the priests to eat (e.g., Leviticus 7:28-36).

29. There are, generally speaking, five types of sacrifices that were offered on the bronze altar: a burnt offering (Leviticus 1:1-17; 6:8-13), a grain offering (Leviticus 2:16; 6:14-23), a fellowship or peace offering (Leviticus 3:1-17; 7:11-21), a sin offering (Leviticus 4:1–5:13; 6:24-30), and a guilt or trespass offering (5:14–6:7; 7:1-6). In this book it is not my intent to explore fully the system of sacrifices, but only to show that the sacrifices on the bronze altar were offered either voluntarily to praise or thank God for his goodness to the people, or out of necessity to atone for or cover the sins of the people. See Hill, 120–121, 287–288, for more details on the offerings.

30. Ezekiel 18:4,20; 33:8; Romans 6:23.

31. The sacrifices of the old covenant were a shadow of the perfect sacrifice of Jesus (Hebrews 10:1). The sacrifices at the bronze altar could never take away sin; they only covered the sins until the perfect sacrifice could come (Hebrews 10:1,3-4,11). This is the meaning of the word *atone* (Hebrew, כָּפַר [kaw·far]), "to cover." Jesus offered his body (his life), not the bodies of animals, as a perfect sacrifice to remove sin (Hebrews 9:11-14; 10:5-10). It is interesting that when John the Baptist saw Jesus he said, "Look, the Lamb of God, who takes away the sin of the world" (John 1:29). Animal sacrifices in the old covenant did not take away sin, they only covered it.

32. See Hebrews 7:27; 9:12,26,28; 10:10. Three of these references contain the emphatic term ἐφάπαξ (ef·ap·ax) in Greek—7:27; 9:12; and 10:10. The term means "taking place once and to the exclusion of any further occurrence, *once for all, once and never again*"; W. Bauer, F. W. Danker, F. Arndt, and F. W. Gingrich, eds., *A Greek-English Lexicon of the New Testament and Other Early Christian Literature (BDAG)*, 3rd ed. (Chicago: University of Chicago Press, 2000), in *Accordance* (Altamonte Springs, FL: OakTree Software), CD-ROM, 1.5, s.v. "ἐφάπαξ."

33. Luke 9:23; see also Matthew 10:38; Mark 8:34; Luke 14:27.

34. Luke 22:42.

35. Genesis 22:1-12. Genesis 22:9 says that Abraham built an altar and placed his son on it as the sacrifice, the burnt offering.

36. Exodus 30:17-21; 38:8.

37. Again, the word here in Hebrews 9:9 is παραβολή (par·ab·ol·ay) in Greek. See note 31 in chapter 4.

38. Hebrews 10:1 literally says that the old covenant sacrifices did not perfect the worshipper (see also Hebrews 9:8-10; 10:1-4). Perfection here has the sense of purifying a worshipper to an extent that he is fit to enter the presence of God in worship. You can also see this theme in Hebrews 7:11,19; 9:9; 10:14.

39. Hebrews 4:15; John 1:14,18; 3:16,18.

40. Psalm 95:10.

41. Jeremiah 17:1,9.

42. Jeremiah 31:33; Hebrews 8:10; 10:16.

43. Hebrews 10:22. This verse uses the verb προσέρχομαι (pros·er·khom·ahee) to describe our drawing near to God. This is a term that is used to

describe those who are drawing near to God to worship him in Hebrews and in the Old Testament. You will find it in this sense in Hebrews 4:16; 7:25; 10:1,22; 11:6; 12:18,22. In the Greek Old Testament (Septuagint) you see this use of προσέρχομαι (pros·er·khom·ahee) in passages like Leviticus 21:17,21; 22:3, which describe the priests drawing near to God to perform their priestly duties.

44. This is one benefit of the fact that Jesus bore our sorrows and griefs upon himself (Isaiah 53:4).

45. Isaiah 61:10.

CHAPTER 6: A MODEL FOR DEVOTIONAL LIFE, PART 2

1. Exodus 13:21-22; 14:19-20,24; 40:34-35,37-38; Numbers 9:15-22; Deuteronomy 1:33.

2. The tabernacle stood 30 cubits long, 10 cubits wide, and 10 cubits high, or roughly 45 feet by 15 feet by 15 feet tall (again, I am basing this calculation on the rough measure of a cubit being 18 inches or 1.5 feet). See Exodus 26:15-30; 36:20-34. For more precise measures see James Strong, *The Tabernacle of Israel: Its Structure and Symbolism* (Grand Rapids, MI: Kregel, 1987), 16. It was covered with three layers of roofing, which were sheets of goat hair (Exodus 26:7-13), ram's skin dyed red (26:14), and on top the skins of "sea cows" (26:14, the Hebrew for sea cow, תַּחַשׁ [takh·ash], means "dugong," a marine mammal, likely a dolphin); see Francis Brown, S. R. Driver, and Charles A. Briggs, eds., *The Brown-Driver-Briggs Hebrew and English Lexicon (BDB)* (Oxford: Clarendon Press, 1906), in *Accordance* (Altamonte Springs, FL: OakTree Software), CD-ROM, 2.0, s.v. "תַּחַשׁ." The last layer served to waterproof the tabernacle and camouflage it from Israel's enemies. See Andrew E. Hill, *Enter His Courts with Praise* (Grand Rapids, MI: Baker, 1993), 169.

3. Exodus 26:36-37; 36:37-38.

4. The Holy Place was 30 feet by 15 feet, and the Holiest of All was 15 feet by 15 feet (Exodus 26:15-25,33).

5. See Ephesians 4:24.

6. See Hebrews 8:3-5; 9:23-24.

7. Exodus 25:31-40; 27:20-21; 30:7-8; 37:17-24; Leviticus 24:2-4; Numbers 8:1-4. Each of the lamp's seven branches contained a bowl at the end, which held olive oil (Exodus 27:20; 37:23; Leviticus 24:2).

8. Exodus 27:21; 30:7-8; Leviticus 24:3-4; 1 Samuel 3:3.

9. We may summarize the different references to light in Scripture under

four headings, using the categories of Dwight M. Pratt:

(1) Natural light is the light God created on the first day of creation.
This light illuminates the earth and gives us the light of day, the light
of stars and celestial bodies, and even the bioluminescence of creatures of the dark. Light is necessary for life in the natural world as we
see in processes like photosynthesis. See Genesis 1:5; Psalm 148:3.

(2) Artificial light is light created by people in their use of materials God
created. Thus, Israel used oil in different kinds of lamps to produce
light in darkness. The golden candlestick is one example of a kind of
lamp. See, for example, Exodus 25:6; 35:8,14; Leviticus 24:2; and in
the New Testament Matthew 5:15 and Acts 20:8.

(3) Miraculous light can be seen in the supernatural acts of God in the
history of his people and in his son Jesus. For instance, the light in
the dwellings of Israel when Egypt was in darkness (Exodus 10:23),
the pillar of fire that led Israel in the desert (Exodus 13:21; 14:20;
40:36-38), the light from the garments of the transfigured Son of
God in Matthew 17:2, and the blinding light of Christ from heaven
in Paul's conversion experience on the Damascus Road in
Acts 9:3 and 22:6.

(4) Figurative use of light in Scripture brings alive images of the spiritual
life of believers. God's Word gives light to believers for the paths of
their lives; this is spiritual direction (Psalm 119:105,130; Proverbs
6:23). Other passages use light as a figure to point the reader to a
"moral attitude to truth" (Job 24:13,16; Isaiah 5:20). Without
"light," people are plagued with a spiritual and moral confusion that
prevents them from discerning right from wrong. We can also see
that life and light are connected from David's words in Psalm 27:1,
"The LORD is my light and my salvation" and the declaration of the
apostle John, "That life was the light of men" (John 1:4). Dwight M.
Pratt offers this fourfold description of light. See Dwight M. Pratt,
"Light," in *The International Standard Bible Encyclopedia*, vol. 3, ed.
James Orr (Grand Rapids, MI: Eerdmans, 1983), 1890–1892.

We cannot mention this fourfold description of light and miss the
references to God as light and Christ as the light of the world. Pratt
summarizes, "Light is an attribute of holiness, and thus a personal quality.
It is the outshining of Deity," (Pratt, 1891). The apostle John says that
"God is light; in him is no darkness at all" (1 John 1:5). While darkness is
a symbol for evil, sin, and death in Scripture (e.g., Psalm 107:10,14;

Proverbs 2:13; 4:19; Ecclesiastes 2:14; Matthew 8:12; 22:13; 25:30), light is a metaphor for holiness, and often for God's holiness and the radiance of his presence (see, for example, Psalm 104:2; Isaiah 10:17; 60:19-20; 1 Timothy 6:16; Revelation 21:23-24; 22:5). Jesus is the light of the world (John 8:12; 9:5; 12:46) and the brightness of God's glory (Hebrews 1:3). In 2 Corinthians 4:4-6 the apostle Paul draws a parallel between the work of the gospel in the hearts of unbelievers and the work of God in creation bringing light out of darkness. In this passage he describes the gospel as "the light of . . . the glory of God in the face of Christ" (2 Corinthians 4:6). Jesus is truly the light of the world, and even his gospel, which brings salvation to the world, is represented as light. It is then no wonder that Jesus calls those who follow him to be the light of the world (Matthew 5:14-16), and he exhorts them to walk and remain in the light (1 John 1:7; 2:10; see also Ephesians 5:8-14).

10. Psalm 43:3-4.

11. John 1:9; 8:12; 9:5; 12:46.

12. Hebrews 1:1-3.

13. John 1:18; 14:21-24; 17:6; Hebrews 1:3.

14. 1 Samuel 3:21.

15. The Psalms provide us with extensive insights into the person of God. To pick only one example, Psalm 145 reveals the greatness of God (verses 3,6), the majesty of God (verse 5), the goodness, righteousness, and compassion of God (verses 7,9,14,18-20), the kingdom of God (verses 12-13), God's faithfulness to his promises (verse 13), and his provision for living things (verses 15-16).

16. See for example: Isaiah 6:1-7; 14:24,27; 40:25-31; 41:10; Jeremiah 9:23-24; 29:4-11; 31:31-34; Ezekiel 36:22-27; Daniel 4:3,34-35; 5:21; 7:13-14; Hosea 3:1; 11:1-12; Micah 6:6-8.

17. Psalm 119:105; Proverbs 6:23.

18. Joshua 1:8; Psalm 1:2-3; 19:7-11; 119:97-99; 2 Timothy 3:16.

19. John tells us, "The Word became flesh and made his dwelling among us. We have seen his glory, the glory of the One and Only, who came from the Father, full of grace and truth" (John 1:14; see also verse 1). The unique revelation of the Father in Jesus, the Son, is also clearly explained in Hebrews 1:1-3 where the fragmented and diverse forms of God's revelation through the prophets is contrasted with the revelation by his Son in the last days.

20. Matthew 11:27; Luke 10:21-22; John 17:6.

21. John 14:26; 1 Corinthians 2:12-14; Ephesians 1:17.

22. The golden table of showbread was on the north side of the Holy Place
    (Exodus 26:35; 40:22-23). It was a table made of acacia wood and
    overlaid with pure gold 3 feet long, 1.5 feet wide, and 2.25 feet high
    (Exodus 25:23-25). Like the other articles of furniture that were
    considered "most holy" it contained rings on the four corners and poles
    to pass through those rings for carrying the table when the camp moved.

23. Leviticus 24:8.

24. The incense represented the showbread and was offered as a memorial
    portion to the Lord by fire on the bronze altar (Leviticus 2:1-2; 24:7).

25. Leviticus 24:9.

26. Deuteronomy 8:2-3.

27. Exodus 30:1-3,6; 37:25; 40:5. Hebrews 9:3-4 states that the golden altar
    was located inside of the Holiest of All. This raises a question for the
    student of Scripture because Exodus 30:6 and 40:26 and the description
    of the altar on the Day of Atonement (Leviticus 16:18) state that the altar
    was in the Holy Place. Of the leading solutions for this issue in current
    scholarship, I would mention three. Harold Attridge suggests that the
    emphasis on the different qualities of service between the Aaronid high
    priests and the Levites as ordinary priests gives sufficient reason for the
    reversal of location of the golden altar. See Harold Attridge, *Hebrews*
    (Philadelphia: Fortress Press, 1989), 238. Paul Ellingworth argues that the
    main concern of the author is not the detailed location of furnishing but
    the distinction between the inner and outer areas as in Hebrews 9:8. See
    Paul Ellingworth, *The Epistle to the Hebrews*, The New International
    Greek Testament Commentary (Grand Rapids, MI: Eerdmans, 1993),
    426, 427. William Lane concludes that the author of Hebrews is follow-
    ing the textual tradition of the Samaritan Pentateuch's recension of
    Exodus, which was available to him. This copy of Exodus would have led
    him to place the golden altar in the Holiest of All. See William Lane,
    Hebrews 9–13, Westminster Bible Companion, vol. 47B (Dallas: Word
    Books, 1991), 220. In understanding ancient texts like the book of
    Hebrews in the New Testament, it is important not to read back onto
    writers of the first-century standards of accuracy from the scientific and
    information age in which we live. The author of Hebrews was concerned
    with presenting our new covenant relationship with God in the terms and
    images of the tabernacle and its furnishings. Details were important to
    him, but not at the level of accuracy expected by twenty-first-century

readers. Attridge's comment is helpful: "It is clear that our text is not alone in placing the incense altar in the inner sanctuary" (Attridge, 235). In 1 Kings 6:22 we read of the golden altar being placed behind the veil in the Holiest of All in the temple. Another reference to the location of the golden altar within the Most Holy Place can be seen in the Second Apocalypse of Baruch 6:7, a work that was written close to the time of the writing of Hebrews, "And I saw that he descended in the Holy of Holies and that he took away from there the veil, the holy ephod, the mercy seat, the two tables, the holy raiments of the priests, the altar of incense." See James H. Charlesworth, ed., *The Old Testament Pseudepigrapha* (Garden City, NY: Doubleday, 1983), 623. It is also important to note that the golden altar is mentioned as a furnishing in heaven itself before God in the apocalyptic vision of the apostle John in Revelation 8:3 and 9:13.

28. Exodus 30:2-3.

29. Exodus 30:4.

30. The sweet incense was a powder made from four substances: Three were obtained from plants (stacte, galbanum, and frankincense), and the fourth from the shell of a mollusk (onycha). They were mixed in equal measure and ground to powder. For more detail see James Strong, *The Tabernacle of Israel* (Grand Rapids, MI: Kregel, 1987), 94–95.

31. Exodus 30:7-8.

32. Exodus 30:10; Leviticus 16:18-19.

33. In Leviticus 10:1-2 we read the story of Aaron's two sons Nadab and Abihu who offered "unauthorized fire" and were burned to death with fire that came out from the Lord's presence. The meaning of unauthorized fire is not explained in the passage. It is clear that Nadab and Abihu offered the incense in a manner that God had not approved. This further illustrates the seriousness of God's holiness, that approach to God is on his terms, not ours.

34. Revelation 8:2-3.

35. In Revelation 8:2-3 John says that the angel at the altar "was given much incense to offer, with the prayers of all the saints." In this passage the prayers of the saints are associated with the smoke of the incense, which goes up before God. In Revelation 5:8, however, the prayers of the saints are the incense: "Each one had a harp and they were holding golden bowls full of incense, which are the prayers of the saints." Thus, in both passages in Revelation the prayers of the saints are associated with the image of incense, either as incense itself or as accompanying the smoke

of the incense up to God. For a more detailed treatment of this passage
see G. K. Beale, *The Book of Revelation*, New International Greek
Testament Commentary (Grand Rapids, MI: Eerdmans, 1999),
454–455, and David E. Aune, *Revelation 6–16*, Word Biblical
Commentary, vol. 52B (Nashville: Nelson, 1998), 511–515.

36. The curtain covering the entrance to the Holiest of All hung between
    four golden pillars (Exodus 26:31-35; 36:35-36).

37. Leviticus 16:2,34; Hebrews 9:7-10. The veil concealed the presence of
    God and marked a system of worship and a period of time in which the
    worshipper could not be purified sufficiently to come into the presence
    of God.

38. Exodus 25:12-13.

39. Hebrews 9:4.

40. In Exodus 16:15 when the Hebrews looked out in the morning and saw
    the manna they said, "What is it?" in Hebrew, מַה־הוּא (mah-hu). This
    phrasing provides a "popular etymology of . . . manna," *BDB*, s.v. "מָן."
    See also note 1 in chapter 2.

41. John 6:48-51.

42. John 6:35-40.

43. Ephesians 3:17.

44. Numbers 16:1-40; 17:1-13.

45. Numbers 17:10. Hebrews 9:4 lists Aaron's rod as one of the three objects
    inside the ark.

46. Remember that God's original desire was that Israel would become a
    nation of priests before him (Exodus 19:5-6). This national priesthood,
    though, was never realized because of Israel's unfaithfulness to God's
    covenant. The priesthood instead was limited to descendants of Aaron
    (Exodus 28:1-4). What Israel limited by their disobedience God restored
    by the perfect sacrifice of his Son and the saving work of the Holy Spirit
    in sealing, indwelling, and sanctifying followers of Jesus. The New
    Testament speaks of believers as royal priests (1 Peter 2:5,9; Revelation
    1:6; 5:10; 20:6), a fulfillment of God's original desire. This dimension of
    our new covenant identity does not appear in the argument of the author
    of the book of Hebrews, though the imagery of the priesthood is used to
    describe drawing near to God in the new covenant. See John Scholer,
    "Proleptic Priests," in *Journal for the Study of the New Testament
    Supplement Series* 49, ed. David Hill, (Sheffield, UK: JSOT Press, 1991),
    127–128. In the book of Hebrews the author's focus is not that Christ

established a new priesthood, but that the old priesthood was no longer necessary because Jesus established a new and living way to God by his perfect sacrifice, which fulfilled and replaced the old system.

47. The word Ἀββά (*ab·bah*) is a term of endearment for "father." It implies an intimate and close relationship as between a child and father (Romans 8:15; Galatians 4:6). See W. Bauer, F. W. Danker, F. Arndt, and F. W. Gingrich, eds., *A Greek-English Lexicon of the New Testament and Other Early Christian Literature (BDAG)*, 3rd ed. (Chicago: University of Chicago Press, 2000), in *Accordance* (Altamonte Springs, FL: OakTree Software), CD-ROM, 1.5, s.v. "Ἀββά."

48. Exodus 31:18; 34:28-29; Deuteronomy 10:2-5.

49. The Law is referred to as "the Testimony," and was placed in the ark (Exodus 25:16,21; 40:20). Specifically, the Testimony referred to the tables of stone containing the Ten Commandments (Exodus 31:18; 32:15; 34:29). The ark is also referred to as the ark of the Testimony, or the ark, which contains the testimony of God's Law (Exodus 25:22; 26:33-34; 30:6,26; 31:7; 39:35; 40:3,5,21; Numbers 4:5; 7:89). Testimony is also used as metonymy (part for the whole) for the ark of the covenant (Exodus 27:21; 30:36; Leviticus 16:13; 24:3; Numbers 17:4,10). The tabernacle was also referred to as the "tabernacle of the Testimony" (Exodus 38:21; Numbers 1:50,53; 9:15; 10:11).

50. 1 Kings 8:9; 2 Chronicles 5:10.

51. Jeremiah 31:33; Hebrews 8:10; 10:16; compare Ezekiel 11:19; 36:26.

52. The ark of the covenant was approximately 3 feet 9 inches long by 2 feet 3 inches in breadth and depth (2.5 cubits long and 1.5 cubits wide and deep). See Exodus 25:10-16; 37:1-5.

53. Exodus 25:17-22; 26:34; 30:6; 37:6-9. Cherubim are celestial creatures that appear in Scripture from time to time. They are composite creatures pictured most clearly for us in the visions of Ezekiel where they are described as having four faces: man, lion, ox, and eagle (Ezekiel 1:10; 10:9-14). For more detail see Strong, 86–90.

54. The Hebrew term for *mercy seat* is כַּפֹּרֶת (kap·po·reth), meaning "propitiatory," or that which appeases God and brings conciliation by the offering of a sacrifice. It comes from the Hebrew verb כָּפַר (kaw·far), "to cover over sin." Thus the Day of Atonement, Yom Kippur in Hebrew, is the day the sins of Israel are covered by the blood of a sacrifice for one year. See *BDB*, s.v. "כַּפֹּרֶת." For the details of the Day of Atonement see Leviticus 16:1-34.

55. 1 Samuel 4:4; 2 Samuel 6:2; 2 Kings 19:15; 1 Chronicles 13:6; Psalm 80:1.
56. See also Exodus 30:6; Leviticus 16:2,12; Numbers 7:89.
57. Leviticus 16:2.
58. Leviticus 16:12-13.
59. See the discussion under the golden altar, pages 182–183.
60. See Psalm 9:1.
61. In Hebrews 13:15 the author uses the word θυσίαν (thoo·see·in), which occurs elsewhere in the book fourteen times referring to sacrifices offered in the tabernacle courtyard (Hebrews 5:1; 7:27; 8:3; 9:9,23,26; 10:1,5,8,11-12,26; except 11:4, which refers to Abel's sacrifice, and 13:15-16, which we are considering here).
62. Numbers 10:33,35; 14:44; Joshua 3:11; 4:7,18; 6:4-13.
63. 1 Samuel 4:13,17-19,21-22.
64. Remember that in chapter 4 (page 45) we showed that the book of Hebrews contains the only New Testament passage that quotes the new covenant prophecy of Jeremiah.
65. Hebrews 4:16.
66. Hebrews 10:19-22.
67. "Enter his gates with thanksgiving and his courts with praise," Psalm 100:4.
68. Hebrews 4:16; 10:19-22.
69. Romans 12:1; also see note 1 in chapter 5.
70. Hebrews 13:16 uses the word θυσία (thoo·see·ah), for *sacrifice* as verse 15 does; see note 61. See also James 1:26-27, which applies another word, θρησκός (thrace·kos), to the service we do to others, especially the vulnerable. *Threskia* refers to cultic rites and the worship associated with them; see *BDAG*, s.v. "θρησκεία."
71. Romans 15:27; 2 Corinthians 9:12; and Philippians 2:25 use the words λειτουργέω (li·toorg·eh·o), λειτουργία (li·toorg·ee·ah), and λειτουργός (li·toorg·os) in Greek, all terms connected with sanctuary worship. Similarly the term εὐωδία (yoo·o·dee·ah), meaning a sweet aroma and acceptable sacrifice to God, is used of the financial gift Epaphroditus brought to Paul from the Philippians in Philippians 4:18. This word is used in the Septuagint for different offerings at the bronze altar (Exodus 29:18,41; Leviticus 1:9,13,17; 2:2,9,12).
72. Drawing near to God is a major theme of the book of Hebrews

and can be seen from the prevalence of terms like προσέρχομαι (pros·er·khom·ahee), "to draw near in worship": 4:16 (believers drawing near to God's throne of grace in prayer); 7:25 (believers who come to the Father in prayer through the ascended Christ); 10:1 (the Old Testament worshippers); 10:22 (an exhortation for believers to draw near to God because of the new and living way opened by Jesus); 11:6 (the one who approaches God must do so with faith); 12:18 (Old Testament worshippers coming to the Mount of God); and 12:22 (New Testament worshippers coming to Mount Zion as a figure of God's presence). See also ἐγγίζω (eng·id·zo), "to come near" (7:19). προσέρχομαι (pros·er·khom·ahee) is used in the Septuagint for the action of priests drawing near to God to perform their priestly duties (Leviticus 21:17,21; 22:3). See also chapter 5, note 43.

73. Hebrews 10:24-25.

74. C. S. Lewis, *The Lion, the Witch, and the Wardrobe* (New York: HarperCollins, 1950, 1978), 172.

75. Jeremiah 7:1-15. See also J. A. Thompson, *The Book of Jeremiah*, New International Commentary on the Old Testament (Grand Rapids, MI: Eerdmans, 1980), 424.

CHAPTER 7: "SISTER JONES KNOWS THE SHEPHERD"

1. *Yaw·dah* occurs 653 times in the Old Testament in a total of 595 verses. It has a wide range of meanings including the ideas of gaining knowledge and understanding, learning to know, knowing by experience, and knowing a person through sexual intimacy; see Francis Brown, S. R. Driver, and Charles A. Briggs, eds., *The Brown-Driver-Briggs Hebrew and English Lexicon (BDB)* (Oxford: Clarendon Press, 1906), in *Accordance* (Altamonte Springs, FL: OakTree Software), CD-ROM, 2.0, s.v. "יָדַע."

2. Genesis 29:5; Exodus 1:8; Job 24:1; 42:11. In Job 19:13 the verb occurs as a participle meaning an acquaintance of Job, or someone who knows him. There are many places in the Pentateuch that describe gods that Israel did not know, e.g., Deuteronomy 11:28; 13:3,7,14; 28:64; 32:17. And of course this word appears describing the action of knowing God through authentic worship in Judges 2:10; 1 Samuel 2:12; 3:7; Hosea 2:20; 5:4; 8:2; Job 18:21; Psalm 79:6. See *BDB*, s.v. "יָדַע."

3. Adam and Eve, Genesis 4:1,25; Cain and his wife, 4:17; of Rebekah as a

virgin, Genesis 24:16; of Judah's relationship with Tamar after she disclosed herself to him, Genesis 38:26; Elkanah and Hannah, 1 Samuel 1:19; of King David not having sexual relations with the Shunnamite, Abishag, who lay with him to keep him warm, 1 Kings 1:4; etc.

4. Psalm 34:8, kjv.

5. I am not suggesting that intellectual or objective means of knowing God are unbiblical or unimportant. These are vital aspects of the discipline of knowing God. I am saying that the relational and experiential dimensions of knowing God are also important, and when they are dismissed or overlooked, our knowledge of God is deficient.

6. John 17:3.

7. Philippians 3:10.

8. This passage is similar to Colossians 1:24 where Paul says that the body of Jesus Christ is still in the world in the lives of his followers who are indwelt by his Spirit. As such, Jesus has not finished suffering in the world. As his followers walk with him and extend his kingdom in the world they will suffer at the hands of a world to which they don't belong (John 15:18-27), a world that is controlled by Satan, the Enemy (2 Corinthians 4:4; 1 John 5:19).

9. In the Old Testament the prophets declared that God's people were destroyed because of a lack of knowledge of God (Hosea 4:1,6; Isaiah 5:13). God did not want his people to merely go through religious rituals, which in themselves were good, but he wanted them to know him (Hosea 6:6). In the New Testament the apostle Paul says that his desire for the followers of Jesus in Ephesus and Colosse was that they would grow in the knowledge of God (Ephesians 1:17; 4:13; Colossians 1:9-10). The knowledge of Christ was worth Paul's losing anything else of value he had (Philippians 3:8). The apostle Peter says the knowledge of God can cause our lives to be filled with grace and peace (2 Peter 1:2), help us discover everything we need for life and godly living (2 Peter 1:3), and help us escape the pollution that is in the world (2 Peter 2:20). Then in 2 Peter 3:18 he exhorts his readers to grow in grace and in the knowledge of the Lord Jesus Christ.

10. The theme of the clay and the potter is a valuable one in Scripture; it is referenced by Isaiah (29:16; 41:25; 45:9; 64:8), Jeremiah (18:4,6), and Paul (Romans 9:21).

11. See the discussion on devotional life, pages 53–55 in chapter 5.

12. Exodus 40:36-38; Numbers 9:17-23; 10:11-34.

13. Numbers 10:33,35; Joshua 3:11; 4:7,18; 6:4-13; 1 Samuel 4:21-22. See also Numbers 14:44 where Israel went into battle without the ark of God.

14. 1 Corinthians 6:19. See 1 Corinthians 3:16 that because of the plural ἐστε (es·tee), it is best taken as the plural "you all together" are the temple of God. For more detail see Gordon Fee, *The First Epistle to the Corinthians*, New International Commentary on the New Testament (Grand Rapids, MI: Eerdmans, 1987), 146–147.

15. Hebrews 10:1 explains that the Law, which in Hebrews refers almost exclusively to the *cultus*, is a shadow of the perfect realities that came to pass in Jesus Christ. In the new covenant the Holy Spirit came to reside within followers of Jesus (John 14:17; Romans 8:9,11; 2 Timothy 1:14).

16. Remember that God revealed his name as Jehovah-Nissi, "the Lord is my banner," when Israel was in battle and Aaron and Hur held up Moses' hands in prayer to win the victory. They came to know him as the God who heals when he purified the bitter water at Marah (Exodus 15:22-26).

17. 1 Thessalonians 5:17, KJV.

18. Revelation 8:2-3.

19. Hebrews 4:16; 10:19-21.

20. Exodus 25:22; 30:6; Leviticus 16:2,13; Numbers 7:89.

21. Hebrews 4:16; 10:19-21.

22. Exodus 25:22; Leviticus 16:2; Numbers 7:89.

23. Numbers 14:6-8; 13:30.

24. John 14:21,23.

25. 1 John 2:4.

26. Exodus 12:29ff.; 14:10-12.

27. Exodus 16:1-2.

28. Exodus 17:1-3.

29. Exodus 14:13.

30. Isaiah 55:8-9.

31. Romans 11:33.

32. Psalm 73:16-17, KJV.

33. Psalm 9:9; 14:6; 46:1,7,11; 48:3; 57:1; 59:16; 62:7,8; 71:7; 91:2,9; 94:22; 142:5.

34. Psalm 27:5; 61:3.

35. Psalm 20:1-2.

36. Matthew 4:4; Jeremiah 15:16.

37. Proverbs 3:5-6.
38. Hebrews 13:15; Revelation 8:2-3.
39. Proverbs 18:10.
40. These passages reveal that the sanctuary, in this case the temple, was the dwelling place of God's name on earth: 1 Kings 8:17,29,43; Psalm 74:7; 1 Chronicles 22:19; 2 Chronicles 20:8-9.

CHAPTER 8: ONE THING HAVE I DESIRED OF THE LORD

1. The Navigators is an international, interdenominational, nonprofit organization that is dedicated to helping people in the United States and around the world discover the wonder and wholeness of a life characterized by knowing Christ and helping others to discover the riches of Jesus Christ in the context of their daily lives.
2. The speaker's name was George Sanchez, and the booklet was *Changing Your Thought Patterns*, which is still available from NavPress.
3. Acts 13:22.
4. In the days of Samuel the tabernacle structure was referred to as "the house of the Lord," suggesting perhaps that there was at least some repair of the original tabernacle by this time (see Andrew E. Hill, *Enter His Courts with Praise* [Grand Rapids, MI: Baker, 1993], 172). During this period of Israel's history the tabernacle structure was in Shiloh (1 Samuel 1:24; 4:3-4). We know that during some of Jonathan's military exploits the tabernacle was still in Shiloh (1 Samuel 14:3). During the reign of David and the early reign of Solomon the tabernacle was at the high place in Gibeon (1 Chronicles 16:39; 21:29). Later David pitched a tent in Jerusalem where he kept the ark of the covenant (2 Samuel 6:17; 7:2; 1 Chronicles 15:1; 16:1; 2 Chronicles 1:3-4) helping establish Jerusalem as Israel's center of worship, but other articles, like the bronze altar, were still in Gibeon (2 Chronicles 1:3-5).
5. David's acquaintance with the tabernacle came in many ways. No doubt Samuel, who was raised as a boy at the temple in Shiloh (1 Samuel 1:3-20,24-28; 2:1-11; 3:1–4:1), and who appointed David king, mentored David in the ways of God from his experience in the house of the Lord. During his perilous days running from King Saul, David ate the showbread of the golden table from the priest Ahimelech at Nob when he and his men were starving (1 Samuel 21:1-6). It is likely that at least some of the tabernacle's furnishings were there during this time. David understood the importance of the tabernacle's furnishings in the worship

life of Israel so much that he had the ark brought back to Jerusalem after
he captured it and set up his residence there on the fortress of Zion,
which came to be known as the City of David (2 Samuel 5:6-10). This
occurred in two stages because of his imprudence in moving the ark from
Kiriath-Jearim in a manner not prescribed by God (2 Samuel 6:1-11).
After David noticed how the house of Obed-Edom was blessed by the
presence of the ark he then had it moved to Jerusalem in a proper manner
and placed in a tent he pitched (2 Samuel 6:12-17).

6. This was not long after David met Samuel. We know that although David
did not know as much as he would later understand about the sanctuary of
the Lord, at this point the Spirit of the Lord had come upon him in power.
Samuel had anointed him (1 Samuel 16:13) and had no doubt mentored
David to some extent because he no longer saw Saul (1 Samuel 15:35).

7. The verb חָזָה (khaw·zaw) is used here meaning to "*look on* (intensely,
with gratification)"; see Francis Brown, S. R. Driver, and Charles A.
Briggs, eds., *The Brown-Driver-Briggs Hebrew and English Lexicon (BDB)*
(Oxford: Clarendon Press, 1906), in *Accordance* (Altamonte Springs,
FL: OakTree Software), CD-ROM, 2.0, s.v. "חָזָה."

8. 1 Chronicles 16:29; 2 Chronicles 20:21; Job 40:10; Psalm 27:4; 29:2;
90:17; 96:6,9; Isaiah 28:5.

9. Makoto Fujimura, *Refractions* (Colorado Springs, CO:
NavPress, 2009), 175.

10. 1 Chronicles 16:29; 2 Chronicles 20:21; Psalms 29:2; 96:9.

11. 1 Chronicles 16:29; Job 40:10; Psalm 29:2.

12. The word כָּבוֹד (kaw·bode) means to "be heavy, weighty, burdensome,
honoured," *BDB*, s.v. "כָּבוֹד."

13. Exodus 40:34-35; 1 Kings 8:10-11.

14. 1 Samuel 23:2,4; 30:8; 2 Samuel 2:1; 5:19,23.

15. See chapter 6, pages 75–80.

16. 2 Samuel 21:1.

CHAPTER 9: THE JOURNEY OF DISCERNING GOD'S WILL

1. 1 Thessalonians 5:18.

2. Luke 22:42.

3. Psalm 62:8.

4. Psalm 34:18; 51:17.

5. Matthew 5:8.

6. Matthew 6:14-15.

7. Ephesians 4:31; Hebrews 12:15.

8. Ephesians 4:26-27,31; Colossians 3:8.

9. Ephesians 5:3; Colossians 3:5.

10. Psalm 119:105. Also, notice how Jesus used the Word of God in his life and ministry. His mission came from Isaiah 61 (see Luke 4:18-22); his discernment in times of temptation came from Scripture (Luke 4:1-13); he validated his ministry and calling in Matthew 11:4-5 by referring to Isaiah 61:1; the spirit in which Jesus carried out his ministry was explained through Isaiah 42:1-4 in Matthew 12:17-21; when he was asked for direction in issues of life, like divorce, Jesus went to Scripture to show people the way (Matthew 19:4-9 refers to Genesis 2:24). Jesus used God's Word to light the darkness around him.

11. It is beyond the scope of this book to offer a theology on the promises of God, but I'll make a few comments on his promises related to the subject of God's will. The promises of God, in many cases, reveal God's intent in the world, and what he plans to do. This is true, for example, of the promises we can trace from Genesis 12:3 to Isaiah 49:6 to Acts 13:47 (where Paul takes Isaiah 49:6 as a mandate for his missionary action) to the picture of the fulfillment in Revelation 5:9-10 and 7:9. We can look to the promises of God to anchor our lives in God's will because his promises reveal many of his purposes in the world, and he invites people into those purposes and uses them to fulfill his desires in the world.

12. Hebrews 11:6; see also Romans 4:20-21 for an example of Abraham and his faith in the promise of God.

13. The book of Proverbs speaks of the importance of counsel in life, business, and war (Proverbs 11:14; 12:15; 15:22; 19:20; 20:5,18; 24:6; 27:9). God often uses other people to carry his messages to his people: Nathan, the prophet, to David after his sin with Bathsheba (2 Samuel 12:1-14); Samuel, the prophet, to Saul (1 Samuel 15:10-35); and Paul, the apostle, to Peter (Galatians 2:11-21). In the New Testament believers are encouraged to speak the truth in love with one another (Ephesians 4:15); gifts of wisdom, knowledge, discernment, and faith are given to the body of Christ for helping one another (Romans 12:6-8; 1 Corinthians 12:7-10; Ephesians 4:11-12). Certainly part of building up the body is giving wise advice to those who are facing important life decisions.

14. James 1:5-8.

15. Isaiah 46:10.

16. Hebrews 4:16; 10:19-21.

17. The tent of meeting: Exodus 30:7-11; the ark of the covenant: Exodus 25:22; 30:6,36 (in each of these verses the Hebrew pronoun ךְ (Kah) [*you*] is singular, indicating God's meeting with an individual); the mountain: Exodus 19:20; 24:1-18.

18. Matthew 12:36; Romans 14:12; 1 Peter 4:5.

19. Ephesians 1:17; see also Andrew T. Lincoln, *Ephesians*, Word Biblical Commentary, vol. 42 (Dallas: Word, 1990), 56–57. We see a similar reference in Paul's prayer for the Colossian believers to be filled with the knowledge of God's will in all wisdom and spiritual understanding (Colossians 1:9), and God's Spirit is the key to gaining spiritual wisdom and understanding (1 Corinthians 2:12-14).

20. Galatians 5:22-23.

21. Acts 16:8-10.

CHAPTER 10: AN ANCHOR FOR OUR SOUL

1. *Hope* in our English Bibles is translated primarily from four Hebrew words: (1) קָוָה (kaw·vaw) (connected with קָוֶה [kaw·veh], meaning stretched out or plumbline), means to be stretched out toward, to long after, or wait for (it is used twenty-six times with God as its object); (2) יָחַל (yaw·chal) means to wait or long (it is used twenty-seven times for waiting on God); (3) חָכָה (khaw·kaw) means to wait (it is used seven times for waiting on God); and (4) שָׂבַד (saw·bar) means to wait or hope (it is used four times for waiting on God). See E. Hoffman, "Hope, Expectation," in *New International Dictionary of New Testament Theology*, vol. 2, ed. Colin Brown (Grand Rapids, MI: Zondervan, 1979), 239.

2. For example, in Isaiah 40:31 the NIV translates the Hebrew verb קָוֶה (kaw·vaw) "hope." But the KJV, NKJV, NASB, ESV, and ASV translate it "wait." Similarly, in Psalm 25:3 the NIV translates the same Hebrew verb "hope," but the KJV, NKJV, NASB, ESV, and ASV translate it "wait."

3. We can see this in the song of the vineyard in Isaiah 5:2. The farmer cleared the land, planted the seed and then he "looked" for the grapes to appear. The Hebrew verb translated *look* is קָוָה (kaw·vaw), to wait or to hope. The farmer expects good grapes to appear because he knows by experience how grape seeds work. He has confident assurance based on his knowledge of viticulture that he can confidently wait on the good grapes to appear.

4. See W. Bauer, F. W. Danker, F. Arndt, and F. W. Gingrich, eds., *A*

Greek-English Lexicon of the New Testament and Other Early Christian Literature (BDAG), 3rd ed. (Chicago: University of Chicago Press, 2000), in *Accordance* (Altamonte Springs, FL: OakTree Software), CD-ROM, 1.5, s.v. "ἐλπίς."

5. Hebrews 10:32-35 speaks about a time in their recent past when the church faithfully endured a great "contest" of suffering. They were publically insulted and persecuted, and some had property confiscated. It also seems clear that their suffering was the background for several of the exhortations in Hebrews, such as the exhortations in 10:35-39 to walk by faith and not shrink back, and others like 10:24-25.

6. Paul Ellingworth, *The Epistle to the Hebrews*, New International Greek Testament Commentary (Grand Rapids, MI: Eerdmans, 1993), 212; William Lane, *Hebrews 1–8*, Word Biblical Commentary, vol. 47A (Dallas: Word, 1991), 153.

7. Hebrews 6:19.

8. Epictetus writes, for example, "We ought neither to fasten our ship to one small anchor, nor our lives to a single hope"; Epictetus, frag. 30. See Lane, 153, for more.

9. The giving of an oath serves as a final confirmation of an agreement or promise. This is a "universal human practice"; see Lane, 151. This passage points us to Genesis 22:16 where, because of the faithfulness of Abraham in sacrificing his son (the account of the *aw·kad*, the offering of Isaac), God reaffirms his promise to Abraham, this time strengthening it with an oath. God swore by himself, because there was none greater than him (Genesis 22:16; Hebrews 6:13). God did this to demonstrate the absolutely irrevocable nature of his promise to Abraham. The divine oath is an absolute guarantee giving the recipient the most possible confidence in the trustworthiness of the promise. See Lane, 151. We also notice in Hebrews 6:17-18 a shift in focus from Abraham to the believers who are the heirs, "we who have fled to take hold of the hope." These believers through Christ have inherited the promise of Abraham. Thus God's purpose for the New Testament believers as heirs of the promise is also "unalterable." See Lane, 152.

10. Hebrews 6:19-20.

11. Hebrews 8:1-5; 9:23-26.

12. Hebrews 9:7.

13. Here the author of Hebrews picks up this theme of Christ's entering the heavens. The theme first appears in 4:14. He will describe it in more

detail in chapters 8 and 9 where he presents Jesus as the superior High Priest of a superior covenant. In the new covenant the perfect High Priest does not enter a tent made by human hands. He enters into heaven itself, which is that to which the human tent pointed (Hebrews 8:1-5; 9:23-26). It was there that he offered a sacrifice that not only perfected the worshipper (Hebrews 10:1-4,11-14), but opened a new and living way into the presence of God in the true Holy of Holies in heaven.

14. Hebrews 12:26-28 tells us that the things which can be shaken—created things—will be removed one day leaving only those things that cannot be shaken. It further tells us that the kingdom we are receiving is unshakeable. The kingdom he has been describing in Hebrews 12:18-27 is a heavenly kingdom. It is also an eternal kingdom (Hebrews 1:8).

15. Psalm 20:2.

16. The Hebrew word here again, תִּפְאֶרֶת (tif·aw·raw), means both beauty and glory. The sense of the word is the beauty and quality of fine apparel and jewelry, which is pleasing to the sight and touch. It also has the sense of the impact of this beauty because of the importance ("weight") of the person wearing it, e.g., the high priest (Exodus 28:2,40) or a king and his regal majesty. We also described this in note 24 in chapter 5. See Francis Brown, S. R. Driver, and Charles A. Briggs, eds., *The Brown-Driver-Briggs Hebrew and English Lexicon (BDB)* (Oxford: Clarendon Press, 1906), in *Accordance* (Altamonte Springs, FL: OakTree Software), CD-ROM, 2.0, s.v. "פָּאַר."

17. Ephesians 3:1-9.

18. 2 Corinthians 12:9.

19. 1 Peter 5:5-6; cf. Proverbs 3:34.

20. Psalm 34:18; see also Isaiah 66:2.

21. 1 Peter 5:10.

22. See *BDAG*, s.v. "ἐλεέω, ἐλεάω."

23. Psalm 86:15.

24. Lamentations 3:22-23, KJV.

25. "Then will I go unto the altar of God, unto God my exceeding joy: yea, upon the harp will I praise thee, O God my God" (Psalm 43:4, KJV).

26. Hebrews 1:3; 2:5-8; 8:1; 12:28.

27. Hebrews 5:9; 9:12.

28. Hebrews 6:16-20.

29. In Hebrews 6:11 the author exhorts his audience to "make your hope

sure." It is clear that God wants his people to be a vibrant picture of hope for the struggling world watching them.

CHAPTER 11: A CROWN OF BEAUTY

1. Paul states this clearly in Romans 3:9; 5:12; Galatians 3:22.
2. We can see this truth beginning with Adam and Eve when they sinned in the garden (Genesis 2:17). Ezekiel states the principle clearly in the Old Testament (Ezekiel 18:4,20), and Paul in the New Testament (Romans 5:12; 6:23).
3. Leviticus 16:9,15-19,34.
4. The book of Hebrews speaks of salvation as a future inheritance (Hebrews 1:14; 5:9; 9:28). We do, however, find another sense of salvation in the book. Because Christ has completed his perfect sacrifice and taken his seat at the right hand of God, a present-tense experience of salvation is also possible. In Hebrews 7:25 both infinitives (σῴζειν [sode·zein] and ἐντυγχάνειν [en·toong·khan·onein]) are in the present tense, which represents the action of "saving" and "interceding" as actions in process, not as completed actions. Jesus is available to help his people when they need it (Hebrews 4:16). See William Lane, *Hebrews 1–8*, Word Biblical Commentary, vol. 47A (Dallas: Word, 1991), 189.
5. Hebrews 9:28.
6. The theology of salvation in Hebrews begins in the opening chapter of the book with a comparison of the unique period of New Testament revelation in Jesus and previous fragmented and diverse forms of revelation through the prophets. This superior revelation in the Son includes the ministry of Jesus as the One who provided purification for sins (Hebrews 1:1-2). The author picks up this theme in Hebrews 2:17 where Christ is called a high priest. The superior high priestly ministry of Jesus, which chapter 7 explains in detail, ushers in a new order of salvation (Hebrews 9:13-15,25-26). See Lane, *Hebrews 9–13*, Word Biblical Commentary, vol. 47B (Dallas: Word, 1991), 218.

    We mentioned in chapter 4 that although the theme of "covenant" is not mentioned until Hebrews 7:22 it is the implicit basis for the comparisons between God's revelation in the Son and the earlier forms of revelation through angels (Hebrews 1:5–2:4), Moses (3:1–4:13), and the high priesthood of Aaron (4:14–5:10). These conversations set up the author's comparison of the salvation provided under the two covenants, the first preparing for and pointing to the second.

In the book of Hebrews the means of salvation is described using the language of sacrifice based on the old covenant system. The author describes sacrifice as that which is necessary for the forgiveness of sins (Hebrews 9:22). The discussion of sacrifice as a means of salvation proceeds along a line of continuity-discontinuity between the two covenants. In both covenants it is a blood sacrifice that deals with the penalty of sin and reconciles people to a right relationship with God.

For the role of sacrifice in the old covenant see Leviticus 16:1-34; Hebrews 7:27; 9:7; for the new covenant see Hebrews 9:15,25-26. See also Lane, *Hebrews 9–13*, 241. Discontinuity lies in the reality that the sacrifices of the old covenant were external and ceremonial (Hebrews 9:7); they could not take away sin (Hebrews 9:26; 10:3-4,11). The sacrifice of Jesus took away sin (Hebrews 9:26,28).

The effectiveness of Christ's sacrifice is another feature of salvation explained in terms of the covenants. The old covenant sacrifices were temporary in that they covered the sins of God's people for only a year. They had to be repeated year after year (Hebrews 7:27; 9:25; 10:1-4). The sacrifice of Jesus, however, was a single, perfect sacrifice for sins, which never had to be repeated (7:27; 9:25-26; 10:10,12).

The result of the "inferior sacrifices" was that the relationship with God established by the old covenant could not purify believers to the extent needed for them to enter the Holiest of All (Hebrews 9:6-10). The old covenant sacrifices were insufficient to qualify a person to enter the Holiest of All. The old covenant relationship between God and his people had to be mediated by the priests. The people did not have direct access to God.

Salvation in the new covenant establishes a new order of relationship with God.

Jesus was qualified to become High Priest of the new covenant and to "come before God in priestly action, he has become the source of eternal salvation to all who obey him (Hebrews 5:9)," Lane, *Hebrews 1–8*, cxlix. Hebrews 2:10 also speaks of Jesus as the "champion" of their salvation, who was perfected through suffering (for a discussion of ἀρχηγός [ar·khay·gos] ["champion"] see Lane, *Hebrews 1–8*, 56–57). The meaning of *perfected* here (τελειόω [tel·i·o·o]) is the idea of going through a process to be qualified to serve as our champion and High Priest. In the Septuagint this term is used for the process of consecrating a priest for his office (Exodus 29:9,29,33,35; Leviticus 4:5; 8:33; 16:32; 21:10; Numbers 3:3). See Lane, *Hebrews 1–8*, 57.

The sacrifice of Jesus for our sins (salvation) was also a ministry of Jesus as High Priest and was carried out in the heavenly sanctuary, not only on the earthly stage of Calvary (Hebrews 8:2; 9:11-12,23-24). The effect of the superior priesthood and covenant is that Jesus in fact cleansed the heavenlies (Hebrews 9:23), which opened a new and living way into the very presence of God in a way no previous sacrifice could. It is beyond my purposes here to delve into the meaning of the cleansing of the heavenly things, which has been widely disputed. Here I simply want to contend that whatever the specific meaning of cleansing the heavenly things, the effect of the cleansing is to open a new and living way to God through the once-for-all sacrifice of Jesus. For two of the best summaries of the interpretive issues see Lane, *Hebrews 9–13*, 247, and Paul Ellingworth, *The Epistle to the Hebrews*, New International Greek Testament Commentary (Grand Rapids, MI: Eerdmans, 1993), 477–478. The sacrifice of Christ perfected the worshipper in that it cleansed the conscience of sin so that the worshipper could approach the Holiest of All, something impossible in the old covenant (Hebrews 9:9,14). This made possible a whole new order of relationship with God (Hebrews 10:19-22).

The mediatorship of Jesus is another place the comparison of the two covenants shines light on our understanding of salvation. *Mediator* (μεσίτης [mes·ee·tace]) refers to a person who "mediates between two parties to remove a disagreement or reach a common goal, mediator, arbitrator"; see W. Bauer, F. W. Danker, F. Arndt, and F. W. Gingrich, eds., *A Greek-English Lexicon of the New Testament and Other Early Christian Literature (BDAG)*, 3rd ed. (Chicago: University of Chicago Press, 2000), in *Accordance* (Altamonte Springs, FL: OakTree Software), CD-ROM, 1.5, s.v. "μεσιτεύω." In Hebrews it is used of a person who serves as the mediator in the formation of a covenant. In all three occurrences of *mediator* (μεσίτης [mes·ee·tace]) in Hebrews the reference is to Jesus as the Mediator of the new covenant (Hebrews 8:6; 9:15; 12:24). Jesus is portrayed as the only Mediator of salvation; see Lane, *Hebrews 1–8*, c.

7. Hebrews 10:19-22.
8. Hebrews 8:10; Jeremiah 31:33.
9. See Hebrews 3:6.
10. Hebrews 2:10-11 express not only the blessing of sonship, verse 10, but also the blessing of being family with Christ, who has made us holy, verse 11.

11. See chapter 4, page 47 (note 20) for more details.

12. C. F. Keil makes the point that while Jeremiah does not explicitly mention the Holy Spirit in the new covenant quotation it is clear from other passages that the Holy Spirit plays a significant and new role in the relationship with God established by the new covenant. See C. F. Keil and Franz Delitzsch, *Jeremiah, Lamentations*, Commentary on the Old Testament, vol. 8, no. 2 (Grand Rapids, MI: Eerdmans, 1982), 40. Notice this theme of the Holy Spirit in the new covenant intimated in these references: Isaiah 59:21; Ezekiel 11:19; 36:26-27. In the New Testament see 2 Corinthians 3:3,6.

13. Psalm 149:4, KJV.

14. The Hebrew adjective here is עָנָיו (aw·nawv), meaning "humble, needy, afflicted, poor"; see Willem A. VanGemeren, *New International Dictionary of Old Testament Theology and Exegesis* (Grand Rapids, MI: Zondervan, 1997), s.v. "עָנָיו." It is the same word used to describe Moses in Numbers 12:3 as the meekest man on earth. In Deuteronomy 8:1-3 the verb form of this word, עָנָה (aw·naw), describes God's work humbling Israel in the desert. It is contrasted with self-sufficiency and pride in Deuteronomy 8:17.

15. The words for beauty and ashes in Hebrew use the same three letters, but in a different order: *ashes* is translated from אֵפֶר (epeh·ayr), and *beauty* from פְּאֵר (peh·ayr).

16. The verbal form of פָּאַר (paw·ar) means to beautify or glorify. See Francis Brown, S. R. Driver, and Charles A. Briggs, eds., *The Brown-Driver-Briggs Hebrew and English Lexicon (BDB)* (Oxford: Clarendon Press, 1906), in *Accordance* (Altamonte Springs, FL: OakTree Software), CD-ROM, 2.0, "פָּאַר."

17. Romans 5:10; Ephesians 2:3.

18. 2 Timothy 2:12; Revelation 1:6; 5:10.

19. Psalm 132:9,16.

20. Genesis 3:21.

21. Genesis 41:42.

22. Esther 6:6-9.

23. Matthew 22:11-12.

24. Romans 6:23.

25. Romans 6:6,11-13,18.

26. Romans 8:29-30; 1 Corinthians 15:50,54; Philippians 3:21.

27. John 1:12; Galatians 3:26; 4:5-6; Ephesians 1:5.

28. Hebrews 10:19-22; 4:16.

29. Colossians 1:13; Hebrews 12:28.

30. 1 Peter 1:3-4.

31. Isaiah 64:6.

32. See Psalm 132:9 and 2 Chronicles 6:41. In Exodus 19:5-6 God expressed his original desire that the whole nation of Israel be a nation of priests. When they failed to keep God's covenant, he shut the priesthood to only the sons of Aaron. This remained the law until the coming of Jesus, the High Priest of the new covenant who was established High Priest not on the basis of human lineage but on the basis of an indestructible life (Hebrews 7:15-16) and with an oath to establish its certainty (Hebrews 7:20-22). Although the book of Hebrews does not develop the theology of the priesthood of the believer, it is explained elsewhere in the New Testament. Peter says in 1 Peter 2:5 that followers of Jesus are "being built into a spiritual house to be a holy priesthood, offering spiritual sacrifices acceptable to God through Jesus Christ." Peter goes on to say they in fact are a holy nation and a royal priesthood (1 Peter 2:9). We also find believers referred to as priests in Revelation 1:6; 5:10; 20:6. Though the sin of Israel caused the priesthood to be restricted, the gracious sacrifice of Jesus opened the priesthood to many.

33. Scot McKnight, "Justice and Righteousness," in *Dictionary of Jesus and the Gospels*, eds. Joel Green and Scot McKnight (Downers Grove, IL: InterVarsity, 1992), 411–412.

34. Colossians 3:10.

35. Exodus 28:2,40, KJV.

CHAPTER 12: THE COMMUNITY OF TRUE WORSHIP

1. Matthew 18:19-20.

2. Galatians 6:1-2; Hebrews 3:13.

3. Ecclesiastes 4:9-10.

4. Exodus 8:22.

5. Exodus 9:11.

6. Exodus 9:26.

7. Exodus 10:23.

8. Exodus 13:21-22.

9. Exodus 14:19-20.

10. Exodus 40:36-38; Numbers 9:15-22; 10:1-12,34; Deuteronomy 1:33.

11. See discussion in chapter 5, pages 55–57, and chapter 6, page 81.

12. Exodus 25:8; 29:44-46.

13. Joshua 18:1; 19:51. In Judges 20:27 the ark of the covenant was at Bethel. By the beginning of 1 Samuel the tabernacle furnishings were back at Shiloh, which was the center of worship for Israel at that time (1 Samuel 1:3,7,9,21,24; 2:28; 4:3-4). The use of the word *house* (בַּיִת [bah·yith] in Hebrew, οἶκος [oy·kos] in Greek), not *tabernacle* (σκηνή [skay·nay]), for the sanctuary at Shiloh leads scholars to think the structure at Shiloh may have been a more permanent structure. See Andrew E. Hill, *Enter His Courts with Praise* (Grand Rapids, MI: Baker, 1993), 172.

14. See, for example, the story of Samuel's calling in 1 Samuel 3:2-14.

15. During the reign of David and the early reign of Solomon the tabernacle was at the high place in Gibeon (1 Chronicles 16:39; 21:29). See Hill, 172.

16. 1 Chronicles 16:39; 21:29.

17. 2 Samuel 6:2.

18. For the conquest of Jerusalem see 2 Samuel 5:6-10. David then moved the ark to the City of David, including an unplanned stop at the house of Obed-Edom after Uzzah was struck dead for touching the ark (2 Samuel 6:2-12). In Jerusalem David set the ark in a tent he pitched (2 Samuel 6:16-17; 7:2; 12:20; 15:25; 1 Chronicles 15:1; 16:1; 2 Chronicles 1:3-4). This tent, which housed the ark of the covenant, was different from the tabernacle of Moses that stood at Gibeon (1 Kings 2:28-30).

19. 1 Kings 8:10-11; 2 Chronicles 7:1-2.

20. 1 Kings 8:12-13,16-17,19,27,29-49. It is clear from Solomon's prayer of dedication that the temple was the place the people of God were to come to meet the God of heaven, especially when they were in need. See also 1 Chronicles 28:2.

21. 1 Kings 9:3; cf. 2 Samuel 7:13.

22. Ezekiel 6:4-9.

23. 2 Kings 15:29; 17:7-17,35; 18:1-12.

24. 2 Kings 25:1-21; 2 Chronicles 36:15-20.

25. Ezekiel 11:16.

26. Ezekiel 10:1-19.

27. See in particular Jeremiah's temple sermon, Jeremiah 7:4-7,9-15. In verse 12 he reminds them of what happened in Shiloh. Israel set up the tent of meeting there and God met his people in Shiloh. But because of the wickedness of Israel, the ark of the covenant was taken from Shiloh by

the Philistines and God's glory departed from Israel (1 Samuel 4:10-11, 21-22).

28. Ezekiel 43:4-7.

29. Ezra 6:13-14; Haggai 2:1-9.

30. Haggai 2:9.

31. Some of the older priests, Levites, and family heads who saw the size of the foundation for the second temple wept aloud (Ezra 3:10-13).

32. Isaiah 1:10. See also Revelation 11:8 where Jerusalem is referred to figuratively as Sodom.

33. Isaiah 1:11-14. The prophet Amos also mentions God's distaste for his people's feasts, assemblies, and offerings and says that he wants to see justice flow down like a mighty river (Amos 5:21-27).

34. Isaiah 58:4.

35. Isaiah 29:13.

36. See Jeremiah's exhortation of the people in Jeremiah 34:8-22, especially verse 14 where he reminds them that the Law requires Jews to free their own countrymen after they have served for seven years.

37. Edward J. Young, *The Book of Isaiah*, vol. 3 (Grand Rapids, MI: Eerdmans, 1972), 420.

38. Isaiah 58:7.

39. Isaiah 58:9.

40. Young, 422.

41. Isaiah 58:9. See Franz Delitzsch, *Isaiah*, Commentary on the Old Testament, vol. 7, no. 2 (Grand Rapids, MI: Eerdmans, 1982), 391.

42. Micah 6:6-8.

43. Psalm 89:14.

44. Francis Brown, S. R. Driver, and Charles A. Briggs, eds., *The Brown-Driver-Briggs Hebrew and English Lexicon (BDB)* (Oxford: Clarendon Press, 1906), in *Accordance* (Altamonte Springs, FL: OakTree Software), CD-ROM, 2.0, "חֶסֶד."

45. See 1 Chronicles 16:34,41; Psalm 36:5; 57:10; 86:15; 100:5; 103:17; 108:4; 118:3-4,29; 145:8; 136 (KJV) in which every verse contains the refrain, "for his mercy endureth for ever." These are only a small sample of the verses that speak of God's חֶסֶד (kheh·sed).

46. *BDB*, s.v. "הָלַךְ."

47. John 14:16-18.

48. The word here in 1 Corinthians 3:1 is νήπιος (nay·pee·os), a very young child, an infant; see *BDAG*, s.v. "νήπιος."

49. 1 Corinthians 3:16-17.

50. 2 Corinthians 6:16.

51. Matthew 18:20.

52. The Holy Spirit is doing on a permanent and global basis what Jesus did on a temporary and local basis. John 1:14-18 describes the Incarnation as the Logos coming into the world and living intimately among us. The word here is σκηνόω (skay·no·o), "to tabernacle or dwell." It is the verbal form of the word σκηνή (skay·nee), the word used throughout the Pentateuch for the tabernacle (see also note 5 in chapter 4). Jesus came and pitched his tent among us, but the Holy Spirit of God lives in the tents of our bodies (1 Corinthians 6:19) and in the temple of the community of God's people (1 Corinthians 3:16; 2 Corinthians 6:16). God literally dwells in his people individually, and as a community in the person of his Spirit.

53. Ephesians 2:21-22.

54. Several of the important manuscripts do not have the phrase "in Ephesus" (ἐν Ἐφέσῳ [en Ef·es·os]) in the opening of the letter (p46, A*, B*, 424c, 1739). It is also absent from Origen's text and other manuscripts mentioned by Basil. This detail, combined with Marcion's comment assigning this epistle "to the Laodiceans," and the fact that neither Tertullian nor Ephraem explicitly quote the phrase "en Ef·es·os" leads scholars to think that this letter was circulated among the churches in western Asia Minor, of which Ephesians was the primary recipient. See Bruce M. Metzger, A Textual Commentary on the Greek New Testament (Stuttgart, Germany: Biblia Druck, 1971), 601.

55. Ephesians 2:19.

56. Ephesians 2:21-22.

57. 1 Corinthians 6:19.

58. 1 Corinthians 3:16-17; 2 Corinthians 6:16.

59. Lincoln also takes πᾶσα οἰκοδομὴ (pas oy·kod·om·ay), "the whole building," in Ephesians 2:21 as a reference to the universal church, making this statement the final of three references to God's dwelling in his people individually, locally, and as a universal body. See Andrew T. Lincoln, Ephesians, Word Biblical Commentary, vol. 42 (Dallas: Word, 1990), 156.

60. Matthew 5:23-24.

61. Matthew 6:12-15.

62. 1 John 4:20-21.

63. Romans 15:27: "They were pleased to do it, and indeed they owe it to them. For if the Gentiles have shared in the Jews' spiritual blessings, they owe it to the Jews to share with them their material blessings." The aorist active infinitive λειτουργῆσαι (li·toorg·eh·o) is translated "to share" in this verse.

64. Philippians 2:30. See W. Bauer, F. W. Danker, F. Arndt, and F. W. Gingrich, eds., *A Greek-English Lexicon of the New Testament and Other Early Christian Literature (BDAG)*, 3rd ed. (Chicago: University of Chicago Press, 2000), in *Accordance* (Altamonte Springs, FL: OakTree Software), CD-ROM, 1.5, s.v. "λειτουργέω."

65. Philippians 4:18.

66. Hebrews 12:28; 13:1-7. The six acts of service are loving one another as brothers and sisters (verse 1); entertaining strangers (verse 2); visiting prisoners (verse 3); keeping the marriage bed pure (verse 4); keeping free from the love of money (verses 5-6); and remembering leaders and imitating them (verse 7).

67. Hebrews 13:16.

68. In a book like Hebrews with such a strong emphasis on the tabernacle worship system it would be impossible to miss the connection between the use of θυσία (thoo·see·ah) here (and in verse 15) and its other thirteen occurrences in the book. Except for its appearance at 11:4, a reference to Abel's sacrifice, the other occurrences of θυσία (thoo·see·ah) refer to either tabernacle sacrifices or Christ's sacrifice, which is understood in light of the tabernacle system.

CHAPTER 13: TRANSFORMATION FROM THE INSIDE OUT

1. Merriam-Webster defines *adore* as "to worship with profound reverence : pay divine honors to : honor as a deity or as divine : offer worship to." *Webster's Third New International Dictionary, Unabridged*, s.v. "adore," accessed May 26, 2010, http://unabridged.merriam-webster.com.

2. See, for example, Proverbs 3:9-10 where honoring God is obeying him by giving out of the firstfruits of one's increase. In Isaiah 58:13 the Lord was to be honored by Israel's obedience to his law regarding Sabbath rest.

3. In Deuteronomy 10:12 עָבַד (aw·bad) is translated by λατρεύω (lat·ryoo·o) in the Septuagint and refers to a "total lifestyle of allegiance to God" (cf. Joshua 22:5; 24:14-24). See Yoshiaki Hattori, "Theology of Worship in the Old Testament," in *Worship: Adoration and Action*, ed. D. A. Carson (Grand Rapids, MI: Baker, 2002), 54. Also note

Hattori's quote of R. Martin-Achard, "Worship," in *A Companion to the Bible*, ed. J. J. von Allmen (New York: Oxford University Press, 1958), 472: "God must be served on all planes of human existence, as biblical legislation testifies. It is significant that Hebrew has one word to denote work, service and worship; in biblical thought there is no watertight division between daily work and the adoration of God; in the very first page of Scripture manual activity and the service of the creator are inseparably linked." See Hattori, "Old Testament Worship," in Carson, 212, note 3.

4. Matthew 4:8-10; Luke 4:5-8. See also the excellent discussion in Hattori, "Old Testament Worship," in Carson, 54–55.

5. The story begins with the fall of Satan from heaven (2 Peter 2:4; Jude 6), which occurred sometime after the creation of angels (Genesis 1:31; Psalm 145:2,5; Colossians 1:16) and before the temptation of Adam and Eve in Genesis 3. In this subversive attack on Adam and Eve in the garden Satan took humanity captive to sin and his dominion of darkness. We can see from Genesis 3:1,4; John 8:44; and 2 Corinthians 11:3 that Satan is the originator of sin; he is also called the "god of this world" (2 Corinthians 4:4, KJV). Jesus refers to the Devil as possessing a kingdom that opposes the kingdom of God (Matthew 12:25-26). The first mention of God's plan to redeem his treasured possession and reconcile to himself many of those who were taken captive by Satan is in Genesis 3:15. God promised to bring the blessing of this redemption to the nations through the seed of Abraham (Genesis 12:3; 18:18; 22:18; 26:4; 28:14; Isaiah 49:6). In the fullness of time Jesus, the Son of God, appeared to take away sin by the sacrifice of himself. The apostle Paul describes salvation in terms of the kingdom in the book of Colossians. Salvation, Paul says, is being delivered from the dominion of darkness into the kingdom of God's Son, Jesus (Colossians 1:13).

One of the clearest pictures of the magnitude and power of God's kingdom is the vision of a stone chiseled out, but without human hands, in the book of Daniel. Although this stone was small, it grew to such enormous size that it filled the whole earth (Daniel 2:34-35,44-45). Jesus picked up this theme in Matthew 11:12 when he described the kingdom of heaven as "forcefully advancing." He also spoke of it in the parables of Matthew 13 when he taught that the kingdom of God is like a seed (Matthew 13:31-32) and like leaven (Matthew 13:33). Whatever else God is doing in the world, he is working in countless ways and places to expand the influence of his kingdom and invite people from every nation to enter it through his Son.

6. 1 Thessalonians 1:8.

7.   Matthew 13:33; Luke 13:21.

8. Mark 5:19; Luke 8:39; Acts 1:8.

9. Romans 1:9,15; 10:14-15; 15:20; 1 Corinthians 1:17; 2 Corinthians 10:15-16; Philippians 1:15-18; 1 Timothy 3:16; 4:13; 5:17; 2 Timothy 4:2; Titus 1:3.

10. Matthew 28:19-20.

11. Galatians 4:19; Colossians 1:28-29.

12. John 15:16; 2 Timothy 2:2.

13. Psalm 22:30; 78:4,6; 71:18; 79:13; 89:1; 102:18; 145:4.

14. Leviticus 11:44; 1 Peter 1:15-16.

15. Hosea 6:6.

16. Romans 12:1.

17. Micah 6:8.

18. The phrase "doing justly" is translated from עֲשׂוֹת מִשְׁפָּט (a·so·vt mish·pat) in Hebrew. It is an action phrase, something that we are to do. This simple noun-verb construction means doing what is right. See C. F. Keil, *The Minor Prophets*, Commentary on the Old Testament, vol. 10, no. 1 (Grand Rapids, MI: Eerdmans, 1982), 497.

19. The word here is חֶסֶד (kheh·sed). See Francis Brown, S. R. Driver, and Charles A. Briggs, eds., *The Brown-Driver-Briggs Hebrew and English Lexicon (BDB)* (Oxford: Clarendon Press, 1906), in *Accordance* (Altamonte Springs, FL: OakTree Software), CD-ROM, 2.0, s.v. "חֶסֶד." This word has a deeper sense of covenantal love, faithfulness, and longsuffering when applied to God's relationship with his people. But in the context of these passages in the Minor Prophets the term is applied to the kind of behavior God expects from his people, extending mercy, kindness, and compassion to others as sacrifices of worship to him.

20. Romans 15:16.

21. The term "priestly duty" is translated from the Greek verb ἱερουργέω (hee·er·oorg·eh·o), meaning to engage in a sacred worship system like the tabernacle of the Old Testament, or to act as a priest. The related noun ἱερουργός (hee·er·oorg·os) means a sacrificing priest. See W. Bauer, F. W. Danker, F. Arndt, and F. W. Gingrich, eds., *A Greek-English Lexicon of the New Testament and Other Early Christian Literature (BDAG)*, 3rd ed.

(Chicago: University of Chicago Press, 2000), in *Accordance* (Altamonte Springs, FL: OakTree Software), CD-ROM, 1.5, s.v. "ἱερουργέω." Another word taken from the world of the tabernacle is the term λειτουργός (li·toorg·os), which Paul uses to introduce himself as a "minister of Christ." The verbal form of this term λειτουργέω (li·toorg·eh·o) is used thirty-seven times in the Pentateuch to describe the priests' ministry at the tabernacle. λειτουργός (li·toorg·os) also appears in the book of Hebrews to describe Jesus as the high priestly minister of the heavenly sanctuary (Hebrews 8:2).

22. This term *offering*, προσφορά (pros·for·ah), appears nine times in the New Testament, including five times in one chapter of the book of Hebrews. In each of the nine occurrences the offering is made in the setting of a sanctuary or represents the death of Christ using sacrifice language from the tabernacle (Acts 21:26; 24:17; Romans 15:16; Ephesians 5:2; Hebrews 10:5,8,10,14,18).

23. Romans 12:1.

24. See David Peterson's explanation of Romans 15:16 in "Worship in the New Testament," in Carson, *Worship*, 70.

25. Philippians 2:17.

26. The two words *sacrifice*, θυσία (thoo·see·ah), and *service*, λειτουργία (li·toorg·ee·ah), are both from the sacrificial systems of the tabernacle and temples.

27. The term σπένδω (spen·do) refers to the drink offerings that were poured out as part of the sacrificial system of the old covenant. See Genesis 35:14; Exodus 29:40-41; 30:9; Leviticus 23:13,18,37; Numbers 6:15,17; 15:5,7,10,24; 28:7-10,14-15,24,31; 29:6,11,16,18,38-39; Deuteronomy 32:38.

28. There is good evidence that Paul also has in view here his own death. For a good discussion of this see Peter T. O'Brien, *The Epistle to the Philippians*, New International Greek Testament Commentary (Grand Rapids, MI: Eerdmans, 1991), 305–306.

29. Hebrews 13:16.

30. 2 Corinthians 9:11-15; Philippians 4:18.

31. *Religion* in James 1:27 is translated from the Greek term θρησκεία (thrace·ki·ah), which frequently appears in nonbiblical Greek literature. It means expressing devotion to deities especially through the use of rites of worship. In Colossians 2:18 it describes worship of angels, but is better translated *religion* in Acts 26:5. While "religion" may capture the general

sense of the word in James 1:27, it is important to note that the central idea of *thrace·ki·ah* is that of worshipping transcendent beings. See *BDAG*, s.v. "θρησκεύω"; see also Douglas J. Moo, *James*, Tyndale New Testament Commentaries (Grand Rapids, MI: Eerdmans, 1985), 86.

32. Matthew 5:16.

33. Exodus 33:14-16.

34. Genesis 17:8; 26:3; 28:13; Numbers 13:1-2.

35. Joshua 2:9-11.

36. Joshua 23:9-10.

37. Psalm 2:4.

38. Psalm 2:1: Acts 24:5; Psalm 2:2: John 1:41; Revelation 11:15; 17:18; 19:19; Psalm 2:7: Matthew 3:17; 4:3; Luke 3:22; John 1:49; Acts 13:33; Hebrews 1:5; 5:5; Psalm 2:8: Hebrews 1:2; Revelation 2:26; Psalm 2:9: Revelation 2:26; 12:5; 19:15; Psalm 2:11: 2 Corinthians 7:15. See Kurt Aland, Matthew Black, Carlo Martini, Bruce Metzger, Allen Wikgren, ed., *Novum Testamentum Graece*, 27th ed. (Stuttgart, Germany: Deutsche Bibelgesellschaft, 1993), 783.

39. For a brief discussion of the messianic nature of Psalm 2 see Peter C. Craig, *Psalm 1–50*, Word Biblical Commentary, vol. 19 (Waco, TX: Word, 1983), 68–69.

40. Psalm 2:8.

41. Genesis 12:3; see note 5 in this chapter for more detail.

42. Hebrews 2:10; Revelation 5:9.

43. 1 Corinthians 3:16; 2 Corinthians 6:16; Ephesians 2:21-22.

44. Notice that in Galatians 3:8 Paul says that God announced the gospel ahead of time to Abraham and then he quotes part of Genesis 12:3.

45. See Psalm 22:27. In the context of Psalm 22 the meaning of "bowing down" is clearly worship. You can see this same theme in Psalm 66:4; 67:3-5; 86:9; and Isaiah 19:21; 27:13; 49:6.

46. See Isaiah 56:7. This verse is quoted in Matthew 21:13; Mark 11:17; and Luke 19:46, though in Matthew and Luke the phrase "for all nations" is omitted. This phrase, though, is present in Matthew's quote, in the Hebrew text of Isaiah 56:7, לְכָל־הָעַמִּים (le·chol ha·'am·mim), and in the Greek text of the Septuagint of Isaiah 56:7, πᾶσιν τοῖς ἔθνεσιν (pas·in tois eth·nes·in).

47. See Deuteronomy 32:8 for a brief explanation of God's work in establishing the boundaries of the nations. See also Acts 17:26.

48. See Revelation 21:3,22; 22:3, which says that the throne of God and the

Lamb will be in the city.

49. Exodus 16:35; Numbers 14:34; 32:13; Deuteronomy 2:7; 8:2,4; 29:5; Joshua 5:6; Nehemiah 9:21; Psalm 95:10; Amos 2:10; 5:25.

50. Exodus 13:17.

51. Klaas Runia, "The Reformed Dutch Liturgy in the Dutch Tradition," in Carson, 109.

52. Miroslav Volf, "Reflections," in Carson, 207.

ABOUT THE AUTHOR

EDDIE BROUSSARD, on staff with The Navigators since 1980, now serves as senior vice president and associate director of U.S. Field Ministries. His responsibilities include influencing and nurturing Navigator ministry culture, helping lead the U.S. field ministries, and championing ethnic diversity and urban and inner-city ministry in The U.S. Navigators. Eddie also holds an MA in New Testament from Trinity Evangelical Divinity School. He and his wife, Barbie, live in Colorado Springs, Colorado.

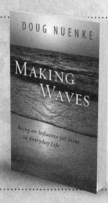

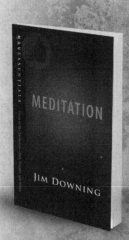  

SUPPORT THE MINISTRY OF THE NAVIGATORS

The Navigators' calling is to advance the gospel of Jesus and His kingdom into the nations through spiritual generations of laborers living and discipling among the lost.

Navigators have invested their lives in people for more than 75 years, coming alongside them life on life to help them passionately know Christ and to make Him known.

The U.S. Navigators' ministry touches lives in varied settings, including college campuses, military bases, downtown offices, urban neighborhoods, prisons, and youth camps.

Dedicated to helping people navigate spiritually, The Navigators aims to make a permanent difference in the lives of people around the world. The Navigators helps its communities of friends to follow Christ passionately and equip them effectively to go out and do the same.

To learn more about donating to The Navigators' ministry, go to **www.navigators.org/us/support** or call toll-free at **1-866-568-7827**.